Text copyright © 2001
by the Resurrection Bay Historical Society.

Illustrations copyright © 2001 by Rebecca Poulson. In sequence, titles of the
wood engravings are: Front cover and chapter 1: "Light." 2: "Old Home on
Beach." 3: "Muskeg." 4: "Snow." 5: "Twinflower." 6: "Boat."
7: "Empty Cabin." 8: "Eagle Bones." 9: "Shipwrights." 10: "Walker."
11: "Winter." 12: "Berry Picker." 13: "Katlian Street." 14: "Cannery Piling."
15: "Fireweed." 16: "Ruined Cabin." 17: "Old Engine."
18: "White Boat." 19: "Looking West."

With the artist's permission, the images have been cropped
and resized for use in this book. The original versions can
be studied at www.theoutercoast.com or by contacting
Rebecca Poulson at 107 Jeff Davis St., Sitka, AK 99835.

The back cover photograph of Elsa and Ted Pedersen
at Bear Cove in 1969 is courtesy of Patricia Williams.

The detail map with the table of contents is adapted from a map of the
Kenai Peninsula drawn by Walt Pedersen, copyright © 1976.

Half of all proceeds above production costs of this book will
go to the Resurrection Bay Historical Society, Seward, Alaska.

Printed in the United States of America.

First printed December 2001.

Hardscratch Press, Walnut Creek, California

Library of Congress Control Number: 2001097078

Cataloging-in-Publication Data

Pedersen, Elsa.
     Kachemak Bay years : an Alaska homesteader's memoir / by Elsa Pedersen ;
wood engravings by Rebecca Poulson.

          p. cm.

     ISBN 0-9678989-1-9

     1. Pedersen, Elsa. 2. Pioneers -- Alaska -- Kachemak Bay Region --
Biography. 3. Frontier and pioneer life -- Alaska -- Kachemak Bay Region.
4. Kachemak Bay Region (Alaska) -- Biography. 5. Kachemak Bay Region
(Alaska) -- History.   6. Women authors, American -- 20th century --
Biography.   I. Poulson, Rebecca. II. Title.

F910.7.P42P42 2001
979.8/3—dc20   2001-097078

                    9 8 7 6 5 4 3 2 1

Kachemak Bay Years

An Alaska Homesteader's Memoir

by Elsa Pedersen

with wood engravings
by Rebecca Poulson

A HARDSCRATCH PRESS BOOK

Books by Elsa Pedersen

— Fiction —

Victory at Bear Cove (1959)

Dangerous Flight (1960)

Alaska Harvest (1960)

Mountain of the Sun (1962)

Cook Inlet Decision (1963)
(U.K. edition *Salmon Boat Sailor*)

Mystery on Malina Strait (1963)

Fisherman's Choice (1964)

Mountain of Gold Mystery (1964)

The Mystery of Kama Lu (1966)

House Upon a Rock (1968)

Petticoat Fisherman (1969)

The Mystery of the Alaska Queen (1969)

— Nonfiction —

The *Alaska* volume of the States of the Nation series (1969)

Kachemak Bay Years (2001)

— Edited and co-published (with Walt Pedersen) —

A Small History of the Western Kenai (1976)

A Larger History of the Kenai Peninsula (1983)

Publisher's Note

ELSA PEDERSEN wrote of her homesteading years at Bear Cove on Kachemak Bay in the mid-1980s and donated the manuscript to the Resurrection Bay Historical Society a decade later; from there it has come to Hardscratch Press. A strong and strong-willed woman, she has been novelist, journalist and historian as well as World War II-era homesteader. It is an honor to be trusted with her recollections.

I met Elsa Pedersen through her "We Alaskans" columns about the Kenai Peninsula in the *Anchorage Daily News* in the 1980s and '90s. I knew nothing of her earlier life in Alaska or of her baker's dozen of books, some of them in second and third editions.

As a memoir of that early period, *Kachemak Bay Years* is compelling reading. But it is more than a personal history. Along with her accounts of the beauty and travail of life on a remote homestead are descriptions of the people and frenzied pace in the salmon cannery where she eventually spent her summers; a riveting account of the 1964 Good Friday earthquake and its aftermath in the town of Seldovia, which would make a book in itself; and a collection of vignettes, some humorous, some tragic, of friends and neighbors and passersby. In a minor key throughout runs the remembrance of years of all-too-human miscommunication and non-communication between two remarkable people.

NEWCOMERS TENDED to pass by, not settle, at isolated Bear Cove, apparently for good reason. I was born and grew up on the Kenai Peninsula, but as with the most incidental tourist my experience of Kachemak Bay is limited to the more accessible, more populated side. Anyone who has driven the last few miles of the Sterling Highway on a sunny late-summer day, over the hill that sweeps down into the colorful community of Homer, with Kachemak Bay sparkling behind it and the peaks and glaciers of the Kenai Mountains as backdrop for the whole peaceful scene, could be excused for failing to comprehend or even consider the often grueling lives of settlers on *either* side of the bay. But at least the people on the Homer side had company.

SELF-DESCRIBED "city girl" Elsa Kienitz was born and reared in Salt Lake City, Utah, where her German immigrant parents, converts to Mormonism, had settled. To the consternation of her family, 23-year-old Elsa took an office job in San Francisco in 1938, after her mother died. In the Bay Area she met her future husband Ted Pedersen, a civilian member of the U.S. Lighthouse Service (now Coast Guard), and went with him to live at Oakland Harbor light station and then at Roe Island, where the Sacramento River joins an arm of San Francisco Bay.

Ted Pedersen (pronounced *Ped*·ersen), 10 years Elsa's senior and the veteran of an earlier marriage, had been born in the Aleutians, son of a Norwegian sea trader and an Aleut-Russian mother who died shortly after his birth. He was cared for at the Methodist-run Jesse Lee Home in Unalaska before being sent at age nine to live with a friend of his father in San Francisco; eventually he spent winters in San Francisco and summers as cabin boy on his father's ship, then when he was 21 joined the Lighthouse Service. His first assignments were in the Aleutians, and when he and Elsa met in California he was dreaming of returning to Alaska. The opportunity came via a job with the Forest Service in Ketchikan; the couple soon moved farther north, first to Seward and then to Seldovia, across Kachemak Bay from Homer. But Ted yearned for wilderness, and there begins this story.

"I had already concluded that there were two types of homesteaders," Elsa Pedersen writes. "One group came to

Alaska as the settlers had gone into the uncivilized American West, to make their homes and fortunes in a place that would eventually develop into a settled part of the country. ... The other kind were those who wanted to get away from civilization and not be drawn into it later. They staked their homesteads mainly to protect themselves from people who otherwise might settle too close. ... Ted and I fitted into this category ...."

THAT THEME and others in Elsa Pedersen's memoir are beautifully conveyed by details from the wood engravings of another Alaskan. Reared in Sitka, where her parents still run the *Daily Sitka Sentinel* newspaper, Rebecca Poulson worked summers on fishing boats and winters repairing fishing boats before turning fulltime to art. She has earned a bachelor's degree in biology from Reed College and a master of fine arts from the Tyler School of Art in Philadelphia; studied for a year at a boatbuilding school in England; and learned wood engraving from famed Alaska artist Dale DeArmond.

In 1992 Rebecca Poulson co-founded the Sitka Shipwrights Cooperative, and since 1994 she has published an annual Outer Coast calendar of wood engravings and poetry. "My prints used to be all boats," she says. "Now they are mostly about the wilderness." Her first child is due the day after *Kachemak Bay Years* is to go to press.

MY IMPRESSIONABLE YEARS were populated with extraordinary Alaskan women. This book is for all of them.

Jackie Pels
Hardscratch Press
November 2001

Contents

ALASKA   CANADA

Kenai Peninsula

ONE

Our Land,
Our Home in Alaska

WE STOOD on the beach to watch the boat pull away and disappear around Moose Point. For long moments the throb of the engine beat against the hills surrounding Bear Cove, reverberating from ridge to ridge until swallowed by the wooded slopes. The date was July 5, 1944.

In the renewed silence of the wilderness we turned away from the mound of freight heaped on the beach. Ted, who had been here before, led the way up the bank to the shelf of forest land that was to be our homestead.

To both of us this was a dream come true. From the time we married we planned to settle in the Alaska wilderness. Just getting there had absorbed all our energies, and to me it seemed a miracle that we had made it in only two years.

1

A creek trickled out of a steep gully, a break in the rocky embankment that surrounded the indentation on the eastern shore of the Cove. The gully and the top of the cliffs were densely overgrown with long-limbed alders that reached for the sun and the beach. We squirmed and fought our way through them to reach the gentler wooded slope above.

The woods looked beautiful to me, mostly gigantic over-mature spruce trees with massive, drooping limbs that made sheltered bowers at their base. The underbrush was spindly spruce saplings stunted in the shadows, rank-smelling elder-berry bushes, and large-leaved devil's club covered with thorns, on the underside of the leaves as well as all along the branches. The earth was thickly coated with moss that absorbed our footsteps. In the silence, with the densely crowded trees and the sweet aroma of the clean air, I felt the wilderness swallow us.

This was *our* land, our home in Alaska we had come so far to claim. Already we envisioned a cabin, a clearing, a garden. We planned to live off the land. Ted had been told that moose were plentiful. Mountain sheep grazed in among the distant mountain peaks, and the waters of the Cove and Kachemak Bay teemed with seafood. We thought we had found Eden.

The hard work started at once. With no dry beach and the larger tides reaching the base of the cliffs, our freight must be moved immediately. Ted hacked a rough trail through the alders and we carried up boxes of groceries one at a time, slipping and sliding precariously. By evening we had taken up everything that would be damaged by the damp. Other crates we wedged among the alders or at the very top of the beach, out of reach of the night's high tide. Too tired to pitch a tent, we dragged one over the cases and crates and crept among them to sleep.

Our enthusiasm was restored by a night's rest, and in the

morning we scouted to find a campsite. Not far from our pile of goods we discovered a small natural clearing near the creek that trickled through the woods. We were grubbing out the underbrush and leveling a tent site when we heard a boat. Peering through the alders we saw the gasboat *Nell,* which had landed us the previous day. Our new neighbors from the fox farm at the mouth of Bear Cove, Harry Leonardt and Paddy Patterson, were aboard. They towed a raft of old logs, part of some dismantled building on the fox farm. They also brought a small hand winch to haul the logs up the embankment so we could use them for our tent foundation.

Harry took charge, with Ted and Paddy doing the work, and they soon erected an enclosure four feet high and 9 x 12 feet in dimension, to accommodate one of our two tents. We had brought some lumber from town and they used 2 x 4s to build a frame on the logs. This provided ample headroom, and the boards we had brought made a floor. When the white canvas tent was pitched over the frame we had a light, airy room as our first home at Bear Cove.

Although we appreciated our neighbors' help, Ted was disappointed with the result. He had wanted to pitch the two tents end to end in one long enclosure, which would have given us more room and spaciousness. I suggested changing before we moved in, but he refused, not wanting to hurt the feelings of the two old men.

"It doesn't matter," I consoled him. "In a few months we'll move into our cabin and use the tents for storage."

We were settled in a few days. Ted made a foundation and floor for the second tent, which would be our bedroom. We had a mattress but no bed springs, so Ted made a crib enclosure which we filled with spruce boughs and twigs. The rest of the bedroom tent space was crammed with duffel bags filled with clothing, and a large plywood box Ted had made in California to ship our bedding, towels and dress clothes. Later we installed a pot-bellied heater Ted found in an abandoned cabin, but we did not use it much.

In Seldovia we had bought a large second-hand cabinet, six feet high and four feet wide, with two front doors and several shelves. This fit in the rear of the living room tent and we used it for household items and things we needed to keep dry, such as stationery and the portable typewriter.

On one side of the cabinet we made a cupboard of stacked wooden cases that each had once contained two 5-gallon cans of gas. These boxes were widely used by homesteaders for chairs, cupboards and other furniture. We used them for storing dishes and tableware and things we used for dining every day—canned milk and sugar, jam, cereal and condiments, and paper sacks filled with beans, split peas, rice and canned goods. On the other side of the cabinet we stored a sack of sugar, sacks of flour and some of our heavier clothing.

Ted built a table with the top of our bedding box, one end resting on the log wall frame, the other on two legs past the middle of the room. We stacked cases of milk against the wall, and used gas cases for seats on either side of the table.

Our stove was a sturdy little cast-iron Shipmate that Ted intended to install in the boat he hoped to own some day. The oven was so small I could bake only two loaves of bread at a time, and Ted had to cut down my baking sheet and turn up the sides of my pie plates. I did not think to use two-pound coffee cans to bake four loaves of bread at once, as did a trapper's wife I became friends with later, who had an equally small oven.

We set the stove on a gas case lying on its side, and kept kindling wood in the case. The stove firebox took seven-inch sticks of wood, which we stored behind the stove. The stove was set in the end of the tent opposite the big cabinet, with the tent door beside it.

We covered the floor boards with tarred roofing paper to cut down the draft, and also to protect the boards, which we intended to use on the cabin roof. The floor space left vacant was so small I swept it with a whiskbroom.

I was delighted with the clean airiness and light of our home. In early July the nights were hardly dark, and in the daytime the white canvas seemed to glow with the light that filtered through the surrounding trees. We worked so hard we had no trouble sleeping, despite the twilit nights. We were both happy and pleased with our prospects as we set about proving up on our homestead.

Although I was a city girl, the wilderness appealed to me. My grandparents had farmed in a remote valley in the Utah mountains and I loved to visit them. When Ted and I met and he proposed moving to his Alaska homeland, I accepted eagerly. My only knowledge of the North came from reading novels by Jack London, Rex Beach and James Oliver Curwood. Listening to Ted's stories of Alaska adventures made me certain we would be happy there.

Bear Cove, the last deep-water harbor at the head of Kachemak Bay on the lower Kenai Peninsula, fulfilled my dreams of Alaska. From where I stood on the edge of the embankment to gaze down over the drooping alders, the sheltered waters seemed like a peaceful mountain lake. The inner cove was additionally sheltered by Moose Point, a long rocky finger of land jutting out from the eastern shore. On the opposite side, a shorter point also thrust out from shore, while a pinnacle rock, covered by the year's highest tides, rose halfway between the points. From outside the mouth of the Cove the wider waters beyond the obstructions were not immediately apparent, so the casual traveler might not realize the presence of the inner cove.

We thought of this sheltered inner cove as our private domain. No other persons had settled there permanently. The wooded slopes rose steeply from the water's edge, ridge behind ridge to a long, barren peak where through binoculars we sometimes saw tiny specks of white that were grazing Dall sheep and mountain goats.

The perpendicular rock walls of Aurora Canyon were silhouetted against the southwest sky back of the sheep mountain, overlooking Portlock Glacier, which was visible from parts of our homestead.

At the head of Bear Cove, between Portlock and Dixon glaciers, was a massive, bare rock mountain we called Flat Top. On either side, sharp-pointed peaks had thrust out of the glacier and slowly grown in size over the years, as the glaciers gradually receded.

We had little time to explore the country, tempted though we were. First we had to clear some land, to get a better idea of how it lay. Once we had cut down trees and brush around our camp we would be able to decide where to build our cabin.

When it came to clearing land, we were both almost literally babes in the woods. Ted had followed the sea most of his life, either aboard ships or on lighthouse stations. I was born and reared in a city; the only roughing I had done was on camping and hunting trips where my father and brother did all the heavy work. Before commencing to fell the gigantic spruce and birch trees, we had a consultation and a minor argument about where on the tree the undercut should be made. We finally solved the problem by studying a stump left by a logging gang two years earlier, when they had cut off the best trees on our future homestead.

Chain saws were not yet in common use when we settled in the wilderness. Our tools were a two-man crosscut saw, a one-man crosscut Ted used to cut the trees in sections once they were felled and limbed, and a bow saw that became my special tool for alders and dead spruce firewood. Ted had a double bit axe and a heavy splitting maul and steel wedges, while I used a Collins single-bit axe for chopping kindling and clearing limbs.

Luckily for our work in the woods, I am ambidextrous. My teachers at school and my mother at home forced me to use my right hand to write and eat, but anything I taught myself was with my left hand. I looked awkward when chopping and sawing, and Ted sometimes laughed at me. My ambidexterity came in handy, though, since I could work with the crosscut saw from either side while Ted was limited to his right hand. When there was a tree to cut in a gully or on a slope and it was awkward for Ted, it didn't matter which end of the saw I handled. I was able to do my share by working on the difficult side.

It was hard for me to learn to saw, however. Although I tried to concentrate on holding the saw straight and level, not to drag my end and not to push the saw on his stroke, sometimes the saw would jam.

"You're bending the saw!" Ted would explode.

If the blade was deep enough in the tree he inserted a wedge behind it to relieve the pressure and we cut again. Otherwise he had to push on the tree with all his might while I wriggled the saw blade free. I always felt guilty when this happened; there was danger the tree would fall the wrong way and make a lot of extra work for Ted.

Some of the spruce trees in the forest around Bear Cove were more than three feet in diameter, punky at the heart and with thick, encrusted limbs as large as young trees themselves. As far as anyone knew there had never been a forest fire around the cove except on Bear Island, and some of the trees dated from the original forest. We tried counting growth rings but gave up after 300.

Clearing land became an obsession. The forest was our enemy. Not only did we have to clear and cultivate 10 acres to prove up on our 80-acre homestead, but we longed for the sun on our eventual home place instead of the overbearing, gloomy trees.

After we had cut down the alders and scraped away many years' accumulation of rotted leaves and grass in the steep-sided gully that contained our creek, we came upon coils of copper tubing and barrels that were rotting away. "So that's where old Jack had his still!" the fox farmers exclaimed when we told them of our find. "We saw him sneaking past a couple of times but could never figure out where he had his camp."

During Prohibition days, bootlegging was practically a cottage industry in some parts of Alaska. We were told that a Seldovia storekeeper got his start making and selling moonshine, while a widow in town supported her family by selling the excellent beer she made. Since the town was a thriving seaport before World War II, ship passengers and crew as well as local residents provided a ready market for illegally brewed liquor.

LIKE OTHER newcomers to the North, we were tricked by the long hours of summer daylight. We thought that when the sun was up we should be outside working. Since in July the sun came over the eastern ridge before five and did not set in the direction of Homer until 16 hours later, that meant a long working day.

Ted went out early to prepare for the day's logging, while I did chores around camp. Right after breakfast we started clearing, expanding our open area a little every day. We started at the edge of the embankment and worked back, across a shelf of gentle slope between the beach and a low ridge to the east.

We worked all day, stopping only for meals, and then

went out again after supper. In a few weeks we had grown weary and muscle-sore. We wondered if we were getting sick. When we realized how we were driving ourselves, we cut down on our schedule. I stayed in camp and did domestic chores or wrote letters in the evening, and the only work Ted did after supper was to tend the fires we built around the larger stumps, to burn them out of the clearing.

Sometimes I went out after dark to sit on a log and bask in the heat of a smoldering stump. The glow of the wood as it burned from flames to embers, the heat that poured out, filled me with a sense of well-being that was hypnotic. I understood why dogs and cats will lie in front of a fireplace, seemingly transfixed by the flames.

To conceal our tents from the Cove, we left two huge spruce trees between our camp and the beach. Ted cut the lower limbs back to stubs that were handy for hanging tools and ropes and gave shelter to some of our other equipment.

One evening a storm blew in. Not the prevailing southwest summer breeze that blew away the insects—this time the wind came in great gusts out of the southeast, roaring down the canyons over the glaciers that are part of the Harding Ice Field. The storm had boiled up in the North Pacific, and it slammed through the passes with the sound of a freight train.

We cowered in bed, watching the canvas press against the tent frame, then balloon out like a sail so that we expected it to carry away momentarily. Ted got up after one great gust to inspect our camp for damage. Moments later he was back. "Come look at this!"

I followed him out of the tent just as another gust roared in from the Cove. He pointed to the two spruce giants we had saved for shelter. Their tops were bending widely, while limbs thrashed like tormented arms. I followed the direction of his pointing finger to the roots imbedded in the moss.

The shallow-rooted trees reared noticeably under the moss, clearly in danger of crashing down on our camp. In the dim light we watched with anxious hearts, until the wind gradually subsided. In the morning our first job was to cut down both of the trees.

Steamboat Jenny
and Others

WE DID not know it when we arrived, but Bear Cove had been the site of an ambitious land settlement promotion in 1903. A group of Finns had formed the Alaska Colonization and Development Company, intending to establish the townsite of Port Axel at the mouth of Bear Cove.

The project included plans to build a sawmill, mine coal from the bluffs of the Homer side of Kachemak Bay, catch and salt salmon and herring, and capitalize on the discovery of oil on the west side of Cook Inlet.

The company sent a work party of three Finn men who spent two years at the Cove and built several log houses. They also cut a wide right-of-way for a road or a tramway that was still visible to us in 1944 as a swath of alders flanked by the primeval forest. After the senior promoter died of a stroke in 1905, the Port Axel project gradually failed, and little was remembered about it when we settled at Bear Cove.

No land titles had been issued to the Finns, and the site of Port Axel was eventually homesteaded by fox farmers Harry Leonardt, his wife Jenny and their partner, W.A. "Paddy" Patterson. They took over the place and lived in the main Finn log house. Jenny had died before we arrived, but she was a legend around Kachemak Bay. It was said that as soon as she spotted a boat coming up the bay she started cooking, and by the time visitors came ashore she had a fine meal on the table.

She was known as "Steamboat Jenny," and Paddy told us why. She was a short but extremely broad and muscular woman, agile on land but awkward and fearful on a boat. One day she planned to go to Seldovia with Harry on the *Nell,* which was moored in deep water in front of the fox farm.

Paddy rowed the two Leonardts from the beach to the gasboat in his skiff. In the process of transferring to the larger boat, Jenny fell overboard. The men struggled mightily to lift her aboard, but with her weight in addition to her watersoaked clothes they could not raise her out of the water. Finally they put a rope around her and Paddy towed her ashore.

"She floated along just like a steamboat," he remarked when recounting the experience to his friends, and thus Jenny received her nickname.

The fox farm made money while she was alive, and the men admitted she had been the driving force. The era of the silver fox boom was the only time the residents of Kachemak Bay truly prospered without leaving their homes to make a living.

We had no idea of how we would survive besides our vague notion of living off the land. We both had dreams of writing but realized that would be a long-term effort and not to be counted on to support us, for the first few years at least.

Like many Alaskans who had come to the Territory during the Great Depression and into World War II, we had no money but were self-reliant. People of our era never forgot the exact state of their finances when they arrived. After Ted and I paid for the groceries, tools and tents we had bought in Seldovia, then bought a sheet of a hundred postage stamps and paid Harry Leonardt for moving us to the Cove, we had 70 cents in our pockets. We felt we wouldn't need money in the wilderness; we had no plans to cope with emergencies but had faith that somehow we would get by.

While we were staying in Seldovia and still looking for a homestead site, Ted ran a boat for C.J. "Kinky" Alexander, who represented an outfit exploring the possibility of starting a king crab processing plant. Ted would set crab pots in a likely area, then anchor up in some bay or cove to give the pots a chance to work. In this way he had come to Bear Cove.

He met Harry Leonardt and Harry's second wife, Lillian, and they showed him promising spots in their area. When Ted chose a place about a mile from theirs they were pleased, and welcomed us to their neighborhood. We spent two nights with them before our supplies arrived, and Lillian said something I was to remember.

"Last night I awakened and realized we have neighbors," she confided as we had breakfast. "*Nice* neighbors."

At the time I was pleased that she approved of me. Later I was sad to realize how lonely she was, the only woman living at the head of Kachemak Bay. I did not know that some day I too would passionately long for neighbors, whether nice or not.

None of us foresaw at the time that we would have little opportunity to develop a friendship. Ted and I were so driven to get settled for the winter, we had no time for sociability. When we went to the fox farm it was on some errand —to take outgoing mail in case someone passed by headed for town, to get some tool left in Harry's warehouse, or to ask for advice, which Ted did as rarely as possible. These trips were always hasty, for if we walked the beach we could get cut off by the flooding tide, and if we went in the waterlogged skiff we had acquired from Harry, it might get stranded and we would have to drag it down the beach to the water.

I really enjoyed going to the fox farm, however brief the visits. To Ted and me it was a model for what we wanted for ourselves on our own homestead. In July the place was in its prime, with lush grass swathing the clearing around the fox pens and white clover blooming in the yard and along the road and paths. Lillian had planted flowers in front of all the buildings, and a strong, healthy lilac bush, more like a tree, stood at the corner of the house.

After our first breakfast together, Lillian had taken me on a tour of her garden, which flourished on a slope facing south, between the house and beach. The beds were raised, bordered with logs and boards to confine the rich, fertile soil. Carrots, turnips, radishes, onions, lettuce, celery and cabbage all grew luxuriantly. Farther down the slope, peas on vines six feet high crawled up the chicken wire staked in rows, with rhubarb and potato patches nearby. Strawberries were just beginning to ripen, while on the steeper slope in front of the house hedges of raspberries grew tall between supporting racks made of dry spruce poles.

Whenever Ted and I went there, we came away laden with garden produce and telling each other we would have a similar garden when we had cleared our land. We did not consider that the fox farm had been settled for a quarter of a century by three hard-working people and usually a hired hand or two. While Jenny was alive they had a cow, a horse and chickens that provided manure to enrich the soil. They also buried fish waste and kelp in plots left fallow for a year or two. The result of all that effort inspired us and spurred us on in our homestead project.

Although we still didn't understand the scope of the undertaking, we began to realize that our glorious adventure had its downright irksome side. The first big problem was insects. Since our land was mostly dry and we usually had at least a little breeze, the legendary Alaska mosquitoes didn't bother us except as a slight nuisance. No-see-ums, tiny winged gauzy flies that were almost invisible until they inflicted their needlelike sting, were harder to bear. They seemed to attack most wickedly in morning and evening, in swarms hard to fight off.

The worst were whitesox flies, which showed no mercy as the day warmed up and we began to sweat. Then these insects, like miniature houseflies but with the white legs that gave them their name, came out of the damp moss and rotten wood and attacked us viciously. Any patch of exposed skin was vulnerable. Although we tied pant-legs and shirt cuffs, covered our heads and necks with kerchiefs, and wore gloves and high woolen socks, they found their way in.

Their bites, in a fold of skin or on thick muscles, appeared as a spot of red that started to swell and itched unmercifully for at least three days. I soon had egg-sized lumps on my arms and legs, and scratched even in my sleep until my skin was raw. Most maddening was when they got under my glasses and into the tender flesh around my eyes. More than once one of my eyes was swollen shut, and the backs of my hands were so swollen the knuckles were buried.

WHEN WE had been in the Cove for six weeks we got a new neighbor. Bill Eklof, a commercial fisherman, bought a small vacant shack across the Cove from us. A bachelor, tall and cadaverously thin, Bill was about my age and 10 years younger than Ted, footloose, talkative and with a vast supply of stories about himself and his offbeat friends.

He lived aboard his little boat *Roamer* and used the shack for storage. It was flimsily built and out of square, and we dubbed it "the tarpaper palace" from the material with which it was sheathed. He had a good creek, larger than ours, and a long stretch of beach, and was outside the inner cove so escaped most of the winter ice. The only thing his spot lacked was winter sunshine, as the slopes cut it off by mid-October. The gloomy winters and loneliness eventually drove Bill away.

I was always glad to see the *Roamer* come across the Cove and anchor in front of our clearing. Bill usually came before supper, and we kept an extra gas case for his seat at the end of the table. I knew we were on his "trapline," as he called those places he visited regularly at Halibut Cove, Peterson Bay, Homer and Seldovia, where he was always sure of welcome and a meal. Like the troubadours in the Middle Ages, Bill paid for his meals with entertainment and small favors, and knew where he was welcome.

I liked his visits for another reason: He always brought our mail when he came from Seldovia. This was no small favor, for we had no regular way of getting and sending out mail. Susan English, postmaster in Seldovia, had a mailbag for each outlying settlement to accumulate letters, magazines and parcel post. Whenever a reliable person from the wilderness came to town, the appropriate sack of mail was sent back with him.

Bill Eklof was our reliable traveler and made the trip to town about once a month. He gave us notice the day before he left so we could finish letters and make out an order for the grocery store. The merchant who had sold us our large grubstake order extended us credit for winter purchases, so we were able to buy eggs, bacon and other perishables, to be paid for the following spring.

After spending a few days along the way and in Seldovia, Bill would appear rounding Moose Point on the *Roamer*, with a great amount of mail for us. Letters from friends and relatives claimed our first attention. We often received packages from them as well, mostly goodies we ordinarily did without.

Next came the magazines. We subscribed to several and greedily thumbed through them and then put them aside to be read in the evenings by the light of our kerosene lamp as days grew shorter.

Reading material was at a premium, and no one threw magazines away. They were read from cover to cover, then circulated among Bill Eklof, the Leonardts and Paddy Patterson, and passed on to travelers who carried them away.

Postmaster Susan English was also in charge of the Seldovia volunteer library. She included packages of books with the mail shipment, knowing we would pass them around and eventually return them in good shape. We had brought a box of books with us from California but stored them in Leonardts' warehouse. We did bring Ted's set of Harvard Classics to the homestead and stored them in the driest place in the living room tent. Over the winter I read many volumes that would not have interested me had I had lighter reading.

On visits to the fox farm I admired and was somewhat envious of the way Lillian and Harry lived, in a modern frame cottage. It was newly built and set on a shelf of land a few hundred feet above the mouth of the Cove. The house was more convenient than any I had lived in in Ketchikan or

Seldovia before we settled at Bear Cove. The front room had hardwood floors, and the soft tones of wall paint reflected Lillian's artistry and good taste. There was running water in the kitchen and bathroom and wonder of wonders, a full-sized bathtub. The only modern convenience lacking was electricity. They did have a small rickety light plant, used mostly to power a washing machine and to charge the radio batteries, but since Harry was not mechanically minded he had trouble keeping it running, and they did not use it for light.

While all these amenities bedazzled me, especially so deep in the wilderness, Ted was not impressed. He admired the log cabin that was partner Paddy's home and thought that it was more in keeping with the natural surroundings. Ever since we first talked of settling in Alaska, he had planned the log cabin he would build for our home. He thought the Leonardt white cottage was out of place in the wilderness, as Lillian also seemed to be.

From the first time I met them I thought the Leonardts an oddly matched couple, and I never got to know them well enough to understand and like them without reservation. As our neighbors they intrigued me, but some mystery always remained.

When we arrived, Harry Leonardt was in his mid-60s, with luxuriant white hair, craggy, ruddy, weather-seamed features and an enormous bulbous nose that dominated his face. He spoke with a heavy German accent although he had left his homeland nearly 50 years earlier.

His manner was of an aggressive certitude that reminded me of my father, also an emigrant from Germany. I was wary of him and so was Ted, for we saw that the old man's word was law around the fox farm and we did not want to fall under his domination. He walked with a rolling gait that at first I thought was a leftover of his years at sea. Later I learned he suffered from extremely painful frostbitten feet.

Lillian was 50, she told me later, slim of build, with iron-gray hair cut close to her head and curled. Her face was handsome, with fine-cut features and a beautiful complexion unusual for a woman who lived in the wilderness. Her gray eyes under black eyebrows studied me intently, and I sensed she was as curious about me as I was about her.

She made me feel clumsy and overgrown, not by intent but because we were so different. At 5 feet 10 inches I was a head taller than she, and my frame was heavy and muscular. While I wore pants and heavy wool shirts every day, Lillian had fine-tailored sport clothing obviously not from Sears or Montgomery Ward, and indoors her dresses were long and elegant, with dainty slippers to match.

We both had been secretaries in San Francisco Bay Area offices when we met and married Alaskans. She and her first husband moved to Anchorage but did not enjoy the then war-crowded town. They moved to a salmon set-net location, then bought an abandoned fox farm near the head of Kachemak Bay, at Battle Creek, several miles from Bear Cove. They spent a winter there, then Lillian took refuge at Bear Cove. She divorced her husband, he left the area, and she married Harry Leonardt. This much, and little more, she told me.

They seemed happy although mismatched, and took good care of each other. One of Lillian's problems, I decided as time went on, was that people constantly compared her with Jenny, Harry's first wife. Seldovia and Homer hunters, who had formerly made the fox farm their headquarters, now came to our place. They told us of Jenny's gusto and her occasional profanity, of her hearty hospitality and the way she ordered Harry and Paddy around. None of this described

Lillian, whom the old-timers found cool and distant. She was criticized for having wanted her own house, although she financed it herself, instead of sharing the large old Finn house with Paddy as Jenny had done. During those two days we stayed at her home when we arrived at the Cove, I recognized something tense and disturbed about her that cast a shadow on our relationship.

THREE

You Can't Build With Green Logs

WE OBSERVED that although the wilderness was peaceful it was by no means quiet. There were always sounds of life—squirrels chattering idly or in shrill alarm if they were disturbed; woodpeckers making tiny tapping sounds as they pecked into spruce bark in search of insects; a high shrill scream of a hawk, or owls hooting to one another across the Cove at night; seabirds squabbling, their quarrelsome sounds drifting into the woods, where twigs snapped under unwary feet, and limbs brushing against a coat could reveal a passer's presence. I had read of hunters moving soundlessly through the forest but learned this is not easily done. Almost every time I have walked in the forest I have been discovered by a blue or gray jay. These birds coast among the trees on silent

21

wings. They are noisy only when alarmed; then their cries set the whole community of birds and animals on the alert and there is no hope of quiet passage until they finally lose interest.

Once we had cleared enough land so we had a view, the sheltered water of the inner cove became our front yard. From the cove the waterfowl chatter resounded all during the daylight hours. Most common were murres, guillemots and scoters, noisy and agitated like quarrelsome children. Cormorants, which Ted called "shags" and Harry called "Norwegian turkeys," fished in the Cove and perched on niches in the rocky outcroppings and on dead trees that had fallen along the embankment and thrust out over the water.

Our favorite seabirds were the loons. Every morning they flew over the Cove from the lake at the foot of Flat Top mountain. On this morning flight they circled the Cove as though on an inspection tour. All the time they sounded their weird, hysterical giggling cry, the basis for the term "loony."

We admired the way they floated on the Cove, paddling strongly but with no visible effort, then signaled a dive by thrusting upward before plunging down with fluid grace. Their evening cry, a long, sad lowing sound, echoed over the woods and water, heralding their return to their nesting lake.

The sleek, round head of a hair seal often broke the surface of the water. These animals followed the salmon up the bay. In later years when I flew over the head of the bay I often saw herds of 200 or more seals lolling on the sand bars at the mouth of Bradley River, waiting for the schools of salmon to come up on the tide.

WE HAD another visiting friend in addition to Bill Eklof —the third partner of the fox farm, Paddy Patterson. In the beginning Lillian had prejudiced me against him, for she considered him her enemy.

"He's a terrible man," she told me when we first arrived. "If I turn my back for a minute he comes into the house. I caught him in the porch when I came up from the warehouse one day."

After the day when he came with Harry to help us build our camp, Paddy stopped by every time he was in our part of the Cove. We found him to be a kindly old man, once tall and strong but now stooped by the hardest kind of labor most of his life. I could not imagine his snooping in the Leonardt house when they were away and decided he must have been looking for some tool on Harry's workbench on the enclosed back porch.

Paddy was the hunter for the fox farm, not only for the people but for the foxes. He had a big old skiff with a cranky outboard motor that refused to start half the time. He had covered the bow with an old piece of canvas that sheltered his ragged sleeping bag. Almost all of every winter he spent his time on the Martin and Bradley river flats, hunting and fishing and trapping for the foxes. He anchored up in a slough in the mud flats, slept in his boat and cooked his meager meals over a Primus stove. His tool box was also his grub box, and uncooked beans and split peas fraternized with rusty pliers and screwdrivers. His life seemed thankless and hard, but he did not pity himself.

He had porcupine traps set all around the Cove and up Martin River, and across Kachemak Bay in the gullies that cut through the sand bluffs. As time went on and Ted and I explored the surrounding hills, sometimes I would get the feeling we were the first humans who had set foot in some remote and secluded spot. Then we would find a tree blaze and a coyote or mink set and know that Paddy had been there before us.

Porcupines were a large part of the fox diet. Paddy skinned them out as soon as he caught them, and Harry told us that Paddy had once nearly lost 200 skinned porcupines when he let his skiff go adrift on the Homer bluff side. Paddy recommended porcupine for eating and brought us one once. Ted was willing to try it but I couldn't bring myself to cook it.

One day Paddy came rowing into the Cove with his fishing seine aboard. A school of silver salmon had gathered off the mouth of our creek, and we helped him make a beach set. He gave us a dozen of the beautiful fish for our efforts. The glass jars we had brought from town were a blessing then, as we added the preserved salmon to our winter larder.

The main part of Paddy's hunting was for moose. No old-time fox farmer would ever admit to feeding moose meat to the foxes, but many of them did. A man who had worked for Harry and Paddy for several years told us they killed at least 40 moose every winter and sometimes nearly twice that many.

In Harry's warehouse we saw a large supply of two-quart jars and a retort pressure cooker, which Paddy told us were used to put up the surplus moose meat to be fed to the foxes in the summer. The salmon they caught were split and dried for future fox feed. Both fish and meat were mixed with oatmeal and cooked in an enormous iron pot over the kerosene stove.

We found it hard to believe that the fox farmers killed so many moose, until some years later when a subsequent owner of the place had an addition built to the Leonardt house. In digging holes for the new foundation, the carpenter came upon a gully that had been filled in and covered over. The whole gully in front of the old original log cabin was filled with moose bones. The bone dump was many feet thick, attesting to the number of animals killed over the years.

Everything about Paddy was ragged and unkempt, in contrast to Harry's appearance of prosperity. It was hard to believe the two men were equal partners. Where Harry was neat and fastidious, his snowy hair trimmed, his ruddy face always clean-shaven, Paddy was the opposite. He may have shaved twice a month, but usually his kindly visage was furred over with stubble. His hair straggled out from under a cap he made from the leg of denim overalls, with a visor cut from the top of a leather boot. His amiable smile exposed gaps in his teeth, and pale eyes blinked through round, steel-rimmed glasses spattered with moose blood, fish gurry and smears from his fingers.

Harry had a small house in Seldovia that he was remodeling, so he and Lillian made frequent trips to town the rest of our first summer. We could always tell when they were gone, for then Paddy came to see us. We urged him to stay for supper and he always brought us something, usually berries or fresh peas or bunches of carrots or turnips.

Like Bill Eklof, he was a storyteller, and he could ramble for hours about his boyhood in Ellensburg, Washington, his years in the Coast Survey, and early days on the fox farm. He told us about his experiences as a cowboy, and once tossed off, "That was the time I broke both arms and both legs," as though it had been an incidental experience. I thought he must have read too many cowboy stories.

Whenever he talked about the fox farm, it was about Jenny. It was obvious to me that he had loved her, too, although she was Harry's wife.

"I did that with Jenny's sewing machine," he told us, pointing to a rough patch on his overalls. "It's the only thing I've got that belonged to her."

Although he spoke freely and often about Jenny, he never mentioned Lillian, neither good nor ill.

We never knew the reason for her hostility toward him.

Paddy had a store of folklore curatives and was eager to share them. He recommended eating a tablespoon of Mentholatum for a sore throat, and a long hike in the woods to cure a cold, and he had a secret remedy for insect bites. When he saw the welts on my hands and my eyes swollen half shut, he assured me his remedy was foolproof.

He brought me a small bottle of thick brown liquid and told me to smear it on my bites full-strength, promising they would stop itching. He was right—the stuff was creolin, which was used, greatly diluted, to disinfect the fox pens. The caustic stuff ate holes in my flesh, so that instead of fly bites I had painful burns on my hands, arms and legs. Luckily I had not tried it on my face.

TED'S MIND was made up to build us a log cabin, despite Harry Leonardt's words of discouragement.

"You can't build with green logs," the old man told us. "No matter how tight you fit them together, when they dry out and shrink you'll be able to throw a cat through the cracks."

Paddy said much the same thing, a little more tactfully. His own log cabin had been put together from logs salvaged from the old Finn buildings built nearly 50 years earlier. He advised Ted to wait until winter to cut cabin logs, as then the sap would be down in the roots. Let the logs season until spring, at least, before starting to fit them into place, he suggested.

My heart fell at his recommendation. It meant that we would have to live in the tents all winter. We had already seen photos and heard stories about snow waist-deep and temperatures below zero. In bad weather, when we couldn't work outdoors, we would be spending more time in the tents, and I was already feeling cramped in our small living quarters. But there was no alternative, and we had trusted to luck many times already. Somehow things would work out for us. Meanwhile, we still had a lot of land to clear.

In clearing land we felled trees with the two-man crosscut saw. When a tree crashed to earth we cleaned the limbs, Ted starting at the stump where limbs were heavy, while I whacked off the smaller limbs at the top.

If the tree was a large one, we cut it in three-foot sections which Ted later split and burned against the enormous stumps. He cut the smaller tips and the smaller trees by himself with the one-man crosscut saw. Burning out stumps proved to be a never-ending and hopeless chore, since one stump could not be burned out with the waste from just one felled tree. I soon learned why homestead clearings were called "stump farms."

I wedged my domestic chores in the times when Ted didn't need my help in the woods. With no real housework to do, my main chores were cooking, baking and doing the laundry. It took me a while to get used to the fast-heating wood stove, and I burned a lot of bread. Gradually I learned to control the heat by leaving the oven door open a crack, and by using slower burning green wood instead of seasoned stuff when I was baking. When I had the time and ingredients I baked cookies, cakes and pies, not only for our own consumption but to have on hand when Bill or Paddy visited.

Laundry was my biggest chore and the hardest work, especially as the weather turned cold. First I carried water from the creek and heated it in a five-gallon can on the stove. Ted had built a little porch in front of the tent and set up a large packing crate to make my washstand.

In a large tin tub I washed the laundry in lukewarm water on a corrugated brass washboard. Almost everything we wore and used was heavy and bulky—flannel sheets, long-sleeved and long-legged woolen underwear, heavy shirts, denim overalls and heavy wool pants in winter. By the time I was finished, the skin on my fingers was usually worn through. I often thought of my mother, who had washed the same way for a family of five and was sometimes not finished when we got home from school in the late afternoon.

In some ways, rinsing was even more painful. Rather than carry rinse water to the tent, I put a tub in the creek, where Ted had built a trough so we could fill our water buckets, and carried the washing to it. Even in summer the water was cold, and in winter, with icy rain or melting snow, it grew even more frigid.

Wringing was an agony, and my hands ached before I was finished. At one time I had had long, slim, supple typist's fingers, but the mistreatment made my knuckles swell permanently. When after several years we sent for a wringer and Ted set it up on a rack over the creek, my laundry chores were a lot easier.

Fortunately, not much of our laundry required ironing. The irons were heated on the stove, and I scorched a lot of pillow cases and blouses before I learned how to adjust the temperature by choosing certain spots on the stovetop where the irons would heat properly. The heavy metal irons came in sets of three of different sizes, with a removable wooden handle. To keep it from charring, the irons were heated without the handle and it was moved from one to another iron as needed. The irons were named "sad irons" for some reason unknown to me, but I thought the name appropriate.

To get a break from clearing land, we sometimes roamed the woods in search of cabin logs. The land we had chosen rose to a gentle crown in the center of our clearing, falling away to creeks on either side. The surrounding woods were a natural amphitheater, the three sides sloping into our clearing. As we made our way through the woods, almost every

12-inch-diameter spruce tree looked like a cabin log. We waited impatiently for cold weather so the sap would go down and we could start logging for our cabin.

As luck would have it, that first winter on the homestead was the mildest we would ever experience. The temperature remained high, and very little snow fell until early spring.

"You don't know how lucky you are," Harry Leonardt told us every time we went to the fox farm. "You've got to get that cabin up."

Since he didn't want us to build a log cabin, we wondered how we could satisfy him. Even if we had the money, lumber was almost impossible to buy in wartime and we had been lucky to get enough for our tent frame and floors. The old man's constant harping got on our nerves and we began to avoid going to the fox farm unless a visit was absolutely necessary.

Because of the mild weather the moose remained in the high mountain meadows and on the distant flats at the head of Kachemak Bay. At least once a week Ted would climb the ridge behind our place and scout the upper Martin River flats, but he never saw a moose.

With the shotgun my brother had given me years earlier for pheasant hunting, I roamed the woods several times a week in search of rabbits and spruce chickens. I was afraid of getting lost—the terrain was irregular, without definite ridges or landmarks—so I never went out of earshot of Ted's land-clearing sounds. That winter we ate rabbit stew, rabbit fricassee, rabbit spaghetti, beans with rabbit. Rabbit was almost our only source of meat and I never enjoyed it again.

FOUR

No Ordinary Storm

IF ANYONE had told me we would spend two winters in tents in the Alaska wilderness, I wouldn't have believed it.

"How could you stand it?" people asked me later.

What could I say? We were in a predicament, but we faced our problems stoically, trusting that somehow we would extricate ourselves. The big problem, I finally decided, was that Ted was a perfectionist. When Bill Eklof, Harry Leonardt, even Paddy urged him to build a temporary shelter, he refused. No shacks for him; he intended to build a fine-crafted log cabin of which he could be proud.

We chose the location just before freeze-up the first winter, on the opposite side of the clearing from our campsite, where one of the small creeks trickled out of the woods. We cleared out a patch of alder behind the new site, and Ted rigged a snatch block high in a large tree so we could haul freight up the creekbed, first using Harry's winch and later our own, our first new piece of homestead equipment.

Ted put in the foundation, using sections of a large seasoned tree he had found in another part of the Cove and floated home. We also searched for smaller dead, seasoned trees to use as the bottom sill logs and floor joists. He flattened the joists on the top to seat the floor boards later. He was a little concerned that the slope behind the foundation oozed moisture but decided he could dig a drainage ditch to divert it.

When we started to cut cabin logs, Ted was highly selective. He rejected many of the trees he had blazed earlier and used only those that were straight and had very little taper. We got most of the logs on the slopes surrounding the clearing, and a few along the edge of the Cove that we skidded into the water and floated home.

Paddy had told Ted that when he had to skid logs he should leave a tuft of twigs on the tip and clean the rest of the tree as smoothly as possible. Fortunately we finally had a little snow, and once we got a tree sliding it went right down the hill to our clearing, the tufted tip weaving clear of trees, boulders and underbrush that could have stopped it.

But getting the tree to slide took every ounce of energy we could muster. With all our strength we tugged on a rope to get the log to the edge of the slope. Then, with Ted prying it forward, I sitting on the ground and pushing the butt end with my feet, we finally got it moving. Ted got so good at aiming the logs that three of them came to rest against the foundation. One went over the embankment to the beach and we had to haul it back up with Harry's winch, as we did the logs we floated home.

In the first warm days of March, Ted started building.

We peeled the logs as soon as we could, then he dressed off the sapwood with an axe and a drawknife. Finally, when the log was smooth and clean, he fitted it in place.

He chiseled a long groove on the under side of each log, to fit it snugly over the one underneath. The corners were cupped to fit over the log that lay at right angles. He used a scribe to mark each log and rolled it back and forth several times to get an exact fit.

While he did this laborious work, I gathered moss in the deep woods where there was no snow. He spread this along the lengthwise groove to bed the logs and over the corners to cut off any draft. By the time he had to go to work in the spring to pay our bills and make a grubstake, the walls of our cabin were waist-high.

Ted had earlier accomplished another task that required a great deal of labor on his part. Since we had no spare lumber for the cabin roof, and our money was depleted, he decided to cut the lumber himself. We scoured the woods for saplings smaller than cabin logs and cut about 30 of them. Ted peeled off the bark and planed off the sapwood. Then he cut every log in half lengthwise with a whipsaw he had traded for the pelt from a coyote he shot on our beach. When he had finished this tedious task he had enough half-round boards to cover the entire cabin roof. He eventually used some of them for rafters and we bought tongue and groove lumber for the ceiling.

During the winter we had met a boat owner who, with his wife, was spending the winter at an abandoned fox farm on Bradley River at the head of Kachemak Bay. Their boat was moored in front of the fox farm at Bear Cove, and the Leonardts invited them and Ted and me to celebrate Christmas. We later hiked up to Bradley River to spend a couple of days with them, and out of these contacts Ted made arrangements for a summer job.

In 1945 the Sterling-Seward highway was on the drawing boards, the exact route not yet decided. One possibility was to build a causeway across Turnagain Arm, from Bird Point on the north side of the Arm to Sniper Point near Sunrise on the south side. A drilling rig was mounted on a scow to probe the muddy bottom. Ted was hired to operate the boat that towed the scow and anchored it in place every high tide. When the scow went dry at low tide the drilling would commence. They drilled at intervals all the way across the Arm, going down 150 feet and finding no bedrock, nothing but sand and silt that would not support a causeway. It was decided to route the highway around Turnagain Arm instead of trying to cross it.

For the six weeks that Ted was gone, I stayed with the boat owner's wife and daughter at the Bradley River fox farm. I had been reluctant to stay alone in the tents while he was away, but now I was happy to return to Bear Cove. Ted went back to work for Kinky Alexander, who had raised more operating capital for his king crab venture, while I remained at home.

When Ted came home in late summer, he was met with the familiar chorus from the neighbors: "You've got to get a cabin built." In my heart I agreed, but I did not tell him how I longed for a roof over my head.

This time he listened. Unwilling to spoil the painstaking work he had already done on the house that was nearly half-finished, he proposed to build another cabin of huge green logs available around the edges of the clearing. He would place this cabin at the top of the rise between the two creeks, and we would later use it for a barn. If he used logs 18 inches in diameter the walls would go up quickly and we would have shelter for the winter.

I was greatly relieved, tired of camping and worried about the condition of our camp. The canvas of the cooktent was dingy and dark. It was getting worn and mildewed where it rubbed over the wood frame, and I wondered how long it would last. The canvas was losing its waterproofing, and when rain fell a fine mist came through.

That was unpleasant, but worse were the swarms of shrews and voles that had begun to invade the cooktent at night. I constantly found little piles of rice and dry cereal they had stolen and hidden in pockets, corners, shoes. A mound of peanuts left in a bowl on the table one night disappeared completely and we never found them.

The damp was pervasive. Our stored shoes, belts and suitcases all grew green and white patches of mildew. The mattress molded on the bottom even though we hauled it out to dry on sunny days. The sugar and flour sacks developed hard casings while other groceries simply absorbed the damp.

All the previous winter we had enjoyed watching a weasel that hung around our camp. We threw out rabbit feet and heads and watched the bold, pretty little animal drag them away. In summer I found his cache. When I emptied the blanket and clothing storage box in the sleeping tent to air the contents, I found the bloody offal tucked into the blanket folds. The little beast had also defecated in the bedding so it all had to be laboriously washed and then aired for days before it lost the disgusting odor.

Kinky Alexander's king crab operation collapsed before the summer was over. Ted had earned just enough to pay our grocery bill and to buy another grubstake, and we faced our second Bear Cove winter with very little money on hand. Ted had confidence, based on lifelong experience, that everything would turn out all right for us. My faith was not so strong but I tried to hide my fears. Meanwhile, we were cut off from knowledge of the outside world. We had no radio, and by the time we got our mail the news magazines were

out of date. The news we got from Harry Leonardt was pes-
simistic, tinged by his inherent fears of Russian expansion-
ism as the allied armies overran Germany from east and
west. When he foretold the Cold War even before the end of
World War II, I accused him in my mind of pro-German
sentiments.

The war with Japan was closer to us. Remembering
roundabout reports of American freighters sunk in the Gulf
of Alaska by Japanese submarines, I sometimes wondered
whether we were also in danger. In the news magazines I had
read of plantations on South Pacific islands being unexpectedly overrun, and wondered what our fate would be if a
Japanese submarine suddenly surfaced in Bear Cove. Ted had
no sympathy for my musings and I quit talking about them.

As luck would have it, we were at least witnesses by ear
to the end of the war. In the first part of August we were surprised by a power scow that came into inner Bear Cove and
anchored within sight of our clearing. Ted recognized the
little floating shrimp cannery of Hank and Lois Kroll. They
had moved their outfit to the head of Kachemak Bay from
Seldovia as Hank explored for new fishing grounds.

Hank was a local eccentric, known all along the southcentral coast of Alaska as "The Mad Trapper." My first contact with him had been within a few days of my first arrival
in Seldovia. We met on the boardwalk, and he confronted
me with the question, "Now who in the hell are you?"

Soon after his outfit arrived in the Cove he rowed ashore,
and Ted invited him to our tent for coffee and a visit. He
told us about the drop of the first atom bomb, but we could
not absorb the significance of that news. He stayed awhile,
rowed back to the scow, and returned a short time later. He
had obviously noted our somewhat austere way of life, for in
a packsack he brought all manner of goodies that he uncere-
moniously piled on our table—cans of fruit and preserves,

catsup, pickles, nuts and candy and a dozen cans of the shrimp he and Lois had put up. I knew that in his rough way he felt sorry for us, and I appreciated his concern.

The scow remained in the Cove several days while the Krolls packed shrimp. One day Hank came rushing ashore to tell us that the second atom bomb of unbelievable force had been dropped on Japan and it appeared that the war was over. At Hank's urging we went aboard the scow and remained far into the night, listening to the radio reports of what was happening in our country and in Japan. None of us could imagine the scope of the event. I remained grateful to the Krolls that we were able to know about the world-altering event, when we had been ignorant of other significant happenings until long after they occurred.

The departure of the Krolls marked the beginning of our second homestead winter. I was happy with Ted's new plan to build some sort of cabin that would be our home until he could build the log house that was his dream. Enthusiastically, therefore, I started to help him on his new project. He set the foundation posts of large green tree butts on the site he selected. The view across the Cove was not quite so grand as from the other site, as we could not see the peaks and glaciers, but we consoled ourselves that this new cabin was only temporary and in a year we would finish and move into the new one on the edge of the clearing.

Luckily, when we had cleared land the previous winter we had left a tall tree near the new cabin site. Ted fastened the winch he had bought to this tree and added a snatch block near the top. With a hundred feet of cable and a choker, we could reach a number of big trees around the edge of the clearing and drag them to the cabin site.

While Ted pried and prodded with a steel crowbar to keep the logs from jamming, I turned the winch handle. Slowly, slowly, the logs crawled down the slope. Just peeling them was a job, and lifting them into place became a major project. My heart was often in my mouth as I ran the winch at Ted's command and he guided each log into place. They were completely green and sappy and weighed hundreds of pounds. He had to roll them back and forth several times before he got them flat enough to fit together. We had bought a bale of oakum to caulk between the logs instead of the moss that old-timers had recommended but Ted found unsatisfactory.

We should have cut all the logs and dragged them to the cabin site before Ted started to build, but this would have meant hitching them to the cable twice, first to drag them to the site and again when we hoisted them into place. To save labor Ted seated each log as soon as we dragged it out of the woods. By the middle of October he had three rounds of gigantic logs in place and we had hopes of being snugly sheltered by Thanksgiving. Then one night it started to snow.

From the beginning we sensed this was no ordinary storm. The snowflakes were as large as feathers and fell with smothering intensity. This early in the season many birch trees and alders still retained their foliage and were soon heavily weighted by snow. Darkness came early. By bedtime we heard trees creaking and crashing. There were sounds of dull thumping as spruce trees became overloaded and the limbs sagged down to relieve themselves of the chilly white burden.

We feared for our tents. The cooktent, although more weak and worn, was the lesser problem. Ted had helped Harry and Paddy get their winter coal supply from the Homer beach, and they had given us part of a skiff-load in payment. We banked the little Shipmate stove for the night, so the canvas stayed warm enough to melt the snow as it fell.

The sleeping tent was our main concern. We rarely used

the heater and had no extra wood on hand for it. As the snow fell the canvas sagged, and the tent was soon in danger of collapsing. Ted set the alarm clock at two-hour intervals and got up to scrape the snow off the roof of the tent so we were not buried in our bed. The snowfall continued for several days, and when it stopped our world was transformed and even more beautiful. Our clearing was no longer an ugly expanse of stumps and the debris of clearing. Instead, it was a beautiful, smooth field of white, the obstructions and clutter concealed. All around the Cove the forest was featureless, with the outline of the trees blurred with the load of snow. Even the Cove was covered, for the snow had fallen too fast to be absorbed by the salt water. The silence was complete, as though squirrels and coyotes, hawks and seabirds all had been smothered by the torrent of snow.

Indoors the aspect was not cheerful. Something had to be done to waterproof the cooktent. First, Harry gave Ted a bucket of old gray paint to seal the pores of the canvas. Now even the faint light that got through the dingy material was cut off. Then Ted borrowed a canvas fly to go over the sleeping tent, so the remaining light was cut off in both tents and they were gloomy inside at midday as well as in the morning and evening.

In the clearing the fluffy snow was waist deep and it was impossible to move out of the dooryard without snowshoes. I was silently heartsick as I gazed upon the building site. The snow was nearly to the top of the third log. Now we had two cabins started, with four-foot walls apiece, and still no roof over our heads.

At first Ted thought we could still cut more trees and finish the second cabin. This soon proved to be impossible. We found it awkward and dangerous to cut down a tree while wearing snowshoes. When we did manage to get one down, it was impossible to drag it through the snow to the cabin site. There was only one thing Ted could do—disassemble the first cabin he had started, and erect it on top of the second. Fortunately he had not spiked the logs together but had pegged them with wooden dowels he had whittled out of seasoned spruce. The biggest job was to tear the walls apart and keep them in order so he could re-assemble them from the bottom in the same way they had originally been put together.

I marvel now at Ted's patience and tenacity. So much had gone wrong with our finances, with his building plans, with his dreams, I would not have blamed him had he said, "To hell with it," and walked away. He was voluble and entertaining when telling stories about his lighthouse and seagoing days, but now he never revealed to me what was going on in his mind. I was equally reticent about my feelings. Perhaps if we had confided in each other we would have exposed discouragement so deep that it would prompt us to give up completely on our homesteading venture.

A Cloth on the Table

WHILE WE struggled with our problems, all was also not well at the fox farm. We didn't know what precipitated it, but Harry and Paddy killed off the foxes and broke up the partnership. Paddy brought us that news and told us the terms. He was to get the fox pelts and a bare building lot in Seldovia. Harry, who unexpectedly claimed Jenny's share as well as his own, would get the property at Bear Cove and the gasboat *Nell*. Lillian had paid for the new house so Paddy had no claim to it.

The house the Leonardts were fixing up in town was apparently also financed by Lillian's savings, so the settlement was not so one-sided as it appeared. Paddy did not complain. He planned to stay in his cabin at the fox farm until spring, he told us, then build a cabin between our clearing and the Leonardts. Harry put a stop to that by ordering Paddy off the place as soon as the transfer papers were signed. Harry declined to move Paddy to town with his meager belongings on the *Nell,* and Paddy had to charter a Seldovia boat to haul his possessions away.

Paddy rented a shack in town and worked on a salmon cannery beach-gang crew the following summer. When the weather turned cold he was stricken with pneumonia. With no doctor in town he was flown to Anchorage, where he died and was buried in an unmarked grave.

We never solved the mystery of Lillian's hatred of Paddy, but it affected our feelings for the Leonardts. Still, with Bill Eklof gone for the winter and the people at Hilmer Olsen's place on Bradley River also giving up, we were the Leonardts' only neighbors. We couldn't stifle a sense of responsibility, especially after Ted went to the fox farm one day and found Harry perched precariously on the roof of his house, trying to clean soot out of the chimney. After that we made it a practice to check on them once a week to make sure all was well, and Ted gave Harry a hand when needed.

Harry always said that as long as he rolled his own cigarettes they would not affect his lungs. He coughed incessantly, until his face grew scarlet, but he didn't stop smoking. That was not his worst health problem. His badly chilblained feet were especially painful in the winter. The only thing that relieved the itching was to soak his feet in very hot water, then plunge them into cold. When we went to his home that last winter we often found him seated with two tubs in front of him, while Lillian constantly renewed the hot and cold water.

Years earlier, before they owned the *Nell,* Harry had set out for Seldovia at the end of autumn in the large packing skiff powered with an outboard motor, to pick up the winter's supply of groceries. He arrived in town without incident, loaded the next morning and was bound for home by noon. A light southwest breeze helped him on his way.

For the first hour all went well. He was approaching McDonald Spit and Yukon Island when the engine sputtered. He made adjustments and it ran a few more minutes, then quit altogether. He could see the breeze was pushing him across the mouth of Kachemak Bay and up Cook Inlet. He couldn't row; the skiff was too heavily laden and the oars were buried under the load. Drifting past Homer Spit he yelled and waved, but no one saw him. In those days the Spit was almost completely deserted by late fall.

He knew that if he drifted to the middle of the Inlet he was doomed. The skiff would swamp, or if by some fluke he made it to the west side of the Inlet there was no place he could take shelter, and he would die on the beach.

At dusk he saw an obstruction ahead. He recognized the Bluff Point fish trap, now only a row of bare poles stuck in the water, the wire fencing and connecting planks removed for the winter. He managed to maneuver himself to the outermost pole and tied the skiff fast with the painter. He didn't trust the skiff. It might break loose or swamp at any time. He crawled up the fish trap pole as high as he could and lashed himself as firmly as possible.

At the fox farm, Jenny and Paddy worried when Harry didn't return on schedule. They had no way of communicating with town. When he didn't show up by nightfall of the day he was expected, Paddy prepared to go to town with their second skiff and outboard motor. He traveled near the beaches, hoping Harry had been forced ashore and was waiting to be rescued.

When he reached town and reported Harry missing, the fishermen went into action. Most of the fishing boats were hauled up for the winter, but the few still afloat took off at once in search of Harry Leonardt. They hunted until dark, failed, and set out again the following daylight.

Harry hung on the trap pole two nights and two days. The skiff had drifted away the first night. Although his body remained dry, at every high tide his feet hung in the water. When the water ebbed, his wet feet frosted until he could no longer feel them. The boat that found him didn't see him at first, tied as he was like a bundle of rags to the trap pole. The fishermen made fast to an inside pole and Harry heard them talking on deck. His tongue was so swollen with thirst he couldn't cry out. Finally he made some weak sounds that attracted their attention.

He was tough and survived the ordeal, but his frosted, brine-soaked feet never healed. Every winter they swelled and the toes split open, and he was lame for the rest of his life.

AFTER THE freakish snowfall the weather turned cold and Ted was also beset by cold hands and feet covered with chilblains as he struggled to finish the cabin. The logs from the original cabin had shrunk and had to be refitted on top of the heavy green wood structure; in cold weather, with very short days, the progress was slow and tedious.

The cold brought another problem. At night our exhalations turned to vapor that froze on the canvas above our bed. During the daytime the temperature sometimes rose above freezing and the frost turned to water that rained on our bed. The bedding became damp and smelled of mildew. The groceries in the cooktent that were stored against the damp walls also began to deteriorate.

It was a happy day in early April of 1946 that we moved into our cabin. It was a simple structure, 12 by 18 feet, with no plumbing and no electricity. To me, however, after living in the tents, it seemed like a mansion. We had headroom! We had windows! We had a floor large enough to sweep with a broom and a roof that did not flap with every passing gust of wind. I was delighted.

In reaction to almost two years of camping, even though our home was a rustic log cabin we had a tablecloth on the table every evening, and used cloth napkins and the silverware I had bought before leaving Salt Lake. I made curtains, got out a bedspread that had been a wedding gift, and otherwise did whatever possible to live with dignity in our wilderness home.

Ted enjoyed our new home as much as I did. He put up shelves and hooks wherever they were needed, brought our books from the fox farm warehouse, and made cupboards for our dishes and groceries.

A short time after we moved in, Ted left for the summer. He had made arrangements to work on a Seldovia salmon seine boat, to fish in Kodiak waters. His dream now was to earn enough money to buy a sawmill, to make lumber out of the logs we cut while clearing land, instead of burning them.

Somewhat to my surprise, I did not mind staying alone on the homestead. In fact, I enjoyed it. The cabin made the difference, for I could lock the door at night and feel secure behind the sturdy walls. I did not wander in the woods, still afraid of getting lost, but I had plenty to do in the clearing. With plans for a vegetable garden, I worked on the patch of alders behind the first cabin Ted had started. My tools were a bow saw and my single bit axe, and I was careful not to injure myself.

Sometimes I rowed around the Cove in the old "Black Demon," as we called the waterlogged skiff. It was hard to row but a good boat to have learned in, as it later was easy for me to row whatever skiff, dory or pram Ted acquired.

I had read about Alaska wildflowers and Ted had told me of the great variety and abundance in the Aleutians. I was disappointed that there were very few at Bear Cove when we first arrived. The woods were so dense that not much sunlight filtered through, and the forest floor was a thick mat of various mosses. There were ferns in the marshy spots along the creeks, and clusters of tiny pink twinflowers, and a few clumps of bluebells and columbine grew in the dirt-filled pockets in the rocks along Moose Point. It was not until we cleared land that we began to see ground dogwood with white blossoms like stars, purple monkshood, and a few clusters of tall Jacob's Ladder.

Whenever I wanted to get away from the place for a while, the boat was my diversion. I also still went to see the Leonardts once a week, as they worried about me alone. At first I rowed, but later I walked the beach. We had discovered that with the exception of a couple of points thrust out from shore that never went dry, we could walk to the fox farm at low tide. By leaving home on the ebb two hours before low water, I could walk to the fox farm, cutting across the rocky points, have time for a visit, and get back home before the flooding tide cut me off.

Once, carrying a packet of letters to be sent out, I rounded a curve and came face to face with a black bear. He was a little fellow and was as startled as I was. When I clapped the packet of mail against my free hand he scrambled up a rockslide and disappeared into the forest.

We had heard that the Leonardt place was for sale, and they confirmed it to me. They were getting ready to move to Seldovia that summer, and it seemed strange to me that Ted and I would soon be the "old-timers" at Bear Cove. When we arrived at the Cove we had thought other homesteaders would soon follow. Instead, the population decreased so that for a short time we and Bill Eklof were the only permanent residents in the entire upper Bay area, at least on the Bear Cove side.

In Conrad Richter's book *The Trees*, he wrote that there were no songbirds in the Ohio Valley until the settlers cleared the land. The same was true of Bear Cove. The first birds we saw when we arrived were gaudy magpies, black, white and iridescent green, that soon made our camp their foraging area. We often heard the mournful cry of great horned owls, signaling to each other from opposite sides of the Cove. Ravens inspected our camp from the air occasionally, making hoarse, rude comments, but smaller songbirds were completely absent.

As soon as we made a clearing, the small birds arrived. Swarms of crossbills and redpolls flew into the giant spruce trees on the edge of the clearing, prying the cones open with their strong bills and feasting on the seeds. Small bands of pine grosbeaks and waxwings appeared occasionally, while woodpeckers pounded so merrily on dead trees in early spring that they sounded like riveters, and we called our place the "Bear Cove Shipyards."

Black-capped and chestnut-backed chickadees depended on the seeds we put out in winter, and juncos, robins and varied thrushes nested in and around the clearing. Spruce hens nested under piles of limbs left from our land-clearing efforts, and I watched them creep stealthily to the nests and fly at full speed when they left.

Two types of birds were especially intriguing—the water ouzel or dipper that ran along the bottom of our creek at its mouth, feeding on waterbugs, and Aleutian wrens that lived in the rocks above the beach in grassy, sheltered pockets.

Both birds had a particularly cheerful early spring song that heralded milder weather. The wrens remained all year around, but the ouzels nested elsewhere.

A pair of kingfishers also spent summers in the Cove, nesting at the end of long tunnels in the embankment in front of the cabin. Their cry sounded like a stick run fast along a picket fence. I enjoyed watching them dive into the Cove and come up with a little wriggling, shiny fish.

In the middle of summer a few seine boats came into the Cove in search of pink salmon. With no large salmon streams and the beaches rock-strewn so that beach seining was difficult, there were no good places to make a set and the fishermen rarely lingered. One exception was the *Nitemare*, operated by an elderly Seldovia couple. They did not fish aggressively, and over the years they made it a habit to visit with me whenever they came into the Cove. If they had fish, they always gave me one.

But visitors, particularly women, remained scarce. While Ted gradually made acquaintance with Seldovians and people who lived at Halibut Cove, I had no such opportunity. I heard stories about many of the people who lived along Kachemak Bay, but I knew very few of them personally.

Ted usually made two or three trips to town in winter, on the *Nell* or on Bill Eklof's *Roamer*, but I had to stay home then to keep the fire going so our canned goods would not freeze. Some years I made one summer trip to town, other years not.

This was a common situation among couples living in the Alaska wilderness. The man got out to trap and hunt, to make the trip to a settlement for mail and supplies, while the woman literally kept the home fires burning.

Ted did not make the good fishing payday he expected. His salmon seining settlement barely covered our grocery bill and our new winter grubstake. For the remainder of the fall he went back to work for Kinky Alexander, who had acquired salvage rights to an abandoned herring packing plant, converted to a salmon cannery, at Tutka Bay, between Halibut Cove and McDonald Spit. He gave Ted the chance to tear down one small building and to keep half the lumber salvaged to pay for his labor.

This was a trait in Ted I had not been aware of: He loved to tear down buildings. In the post-war period when new lumber was scarce and costly, I was as pleased as he was with the siding, shiplap and dimensional lumber he brought home. Even before we moved into our cabin he had talked of the comfortable, modern home he planned to build some day. The used lumber he brought home made me think we could soon start building.

By this time Ted had lost his desire to build our permanent home of logs. Since the lower logs in our cabin were green when he put them together, as Harry Leonardt had warned they shrank as they seasoned—not enough to "throw a cat through," but enough to admit drafts that made long fingers of frost in the cabin and caused the front window casing to hang up on the top log as the walls settled around the window frame.

I had retained my admiration of Lillian's snug cottage at the fox farm and hoped in my heart of hearts that with the lumber Ted salvaged he would build a home as soon as we could afford to buy windows, plumbing supplies, and other building materials.

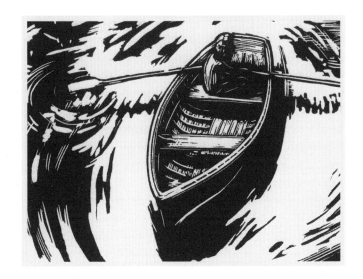

SIX

'The Way to Learn to Write is
To Write'

THE FALL of 1946 began a population explosion at Bear Cove. After Leonardts left, Bill Eklof was our only neighbor for a while. Suddenly we had people all over the place. A couple from Fairbanks and their small daughter bought the fox farm. When they moved in, they were accompanied by another couple we mistook for partners, who remained for several months. More people were to follow.

Bill Eklof brought the news that a couple from Michigan, Frank and Gertie Kuzma, and their two little daughters had moved into an old log cabin halfway between the Cove and Martin River, on the mainland near Indian Island. They were looking for homestead land, planning to settle in the wilderness.

Then early one morning, while Ted was drinking coffee and gazing out the window and I was still in bed, I heard him exclaim, then rush out of the cabin and down to the beach. Moments later he yelled and someone answered. Hastily I dressed and threw the bedding together. Our single room was bedroom, living room and kitchen combined, and I made it and myself presentable as Ted ushered in a stranger.

Over breakfast, Tuggle Int-Hout told us that he, his brother Pierre and a friend, Joe, had come from Illinois, spent the summer in Fairbanks and then wandered down to the Kenai Peninsula. They planned to build a shack and spend the winter hunting, trapping and prospecting. Suddenly the population of Bear Cove had burgeoned to 15, plus another trapper who moved into the cabin at Battle Creek up the bay from Martin River, where Lillian Leonardt had lived when she first came into the country. I was excited about this, especially since the newcomers included three women.

The first to leave was would-be prospector Joe, but the Int-Hout brothers stayed. They built a ramshackle cabin on Martin Spit, using small logs with the old windows, boards, nails and corrugated tin for the roof that Ted gave them. I helped out with a few pots, pans and dishes, towels and dishtowels. I even threw in a couple of potholders which Tuggle returned as too sissified to be seen in a bachelor cabin. We liked them and did all we could to encourage them to stay.

The visiting couple at the fox farm were the next to leave, deciding that wilderness life was not for them. They went back to Fairbanks. The new owners were long on enthusiasm but short on the skills they needed to survive. The man's smugness and superior attitude despite his inability to cope with the simplest problems soon infuriated Ted, and we saw very little of them except when they needed help with the *Nell* and asked Ted's advice.

The Kuzmas were a different story, and Gertie became the best friend I ever had at Bear Cove. We were a long time getting acquainted. They lived more than two miles from us through rough and untracked forest. I did not dare to try to hike to her place without a blazed trail to guide me. Bill had already made friends with them and brought Frank to see us, but like other wilderness wives Gertie was tied to the cabin, in her case by a tiny baby and a little girl. When Ted and I hiked through the woods to see her, she and I became friends immediately and wished we could see each other more often.

The winter before had been the Big Snow Year, and the year following was the coldest winter on record in the Kachemak Bay area. With very little snow on the ground, the cold clamped down early in November. The whole country froze up. Every ebbing tide left a coat of ice on the beach. These laminations continued twice every 24 hours until an ice shelf six feet deep formed all around our beach and halfway to the tip of Moose Point.

Sheltered by the hills and the out-thrust points, the surface of inner Bear Cove became a sheet of ice, broken on the edges where it chafed against the shore at low tide. The middle was a solid pan with the exception of more broken ice around the rock in the middle of the entrance to the inner cove.

Our creeks froze solid to the bottom and we chopped ice and melted it for water until Ted found an ever-flowing spring in the forest behind our clearing. Every night when the cold pressed down we heard birch trees explode as the sap in the trunks froze and expanded, splitting the trees from top to bottom. More than once I gave thanks that we were in the cabin. I was sure we could not have survived in the tents through that bitterly cold winter. No wonder the neighbors had worried about us, and nagged us to build a cabin.

It was too cold to try to clear land or to do carpenter work outdoors. An axe blade would break, crystalized by the cold, and the trees were frozen too solid to cut easily. Ted couldn't do carpenter work without gloves, and that would be impossibly awkward. With a clear conscience, he played all winter. He and the Int-Hout brothers became kindred spirits, roving the forests and mountains. This was Ted's first real chance to explore the back country, and he made the most of it.

There never was a better time to roam over the land. All the foliage was gone from the underbrush. The swamps, the ponds, the moss on the forest floor all were frozen solid. It was easy to walk anywhere, with spiked creepers or crampons to maintain a foothold. Martin River was frozen completely, making a smooth, icy highway to the mountains. Even the rapids were frozen.

I went once with the three of them up Martin River Canyon, to recover the rest of the Dall sheep they had shot the previous day. Bundled against the cold, with a muffler to protect my nose and mouth, I followed Ted over the ridge behind our place, crunching through swampy meadows and willows to Martin River where we met Tuggle and Pierre.

Ted had learned on previous hikes that without landmarks it was hard to find the place to turn off the river and head over the ridge after dark on these short winter days. He carried our lantern, lit it and hung it on a handy tree when we reached the river. On our homeward hike it was a beacon to show us where to leave the river and head up the trail to the ridge.

Our metal creepers rang in the cold air as we kicked against rocks sticking out of the ice. We made good time and were happy in the sunshine despite the frigid weather. Approaching the mountains we entered the shadows, and immediately the cold clamped down. The stream made a sharp turn, then another, and suddenly we were in a gorge deep in the mountains.

This route would be impassable in summer when Martin River filled the entire bottom of the canyon. The passage grew so narrow our arms spanned from one side of the cliffs to the other. The stream bed grew steeper, but even the waterfalls were glazed solid, although we could see water running under the clear ice. As we scrambled upward seeking hand and toeholds on the slick surface our main concern was not to break through, for to get wet would be fatal.

Ahead the way straightened and we saw sunshine. The canyon widened into a quiet, sheltered, sun-flooded bowl, with a massive glacier at its head. As we approached the wall of ice and I gazed at its face, I was awestruck at the thought that we were in the presence of the last Ice Age.

This hike was the exception. Usually I stayed home, baking cookies and brownies, bread, cakes and pies for the appreciation of the men when they came in from their expeditions. The boys occasionally stayed overnight to get an early start on one of their hikes. They slept on the floor, and our cabin no longer seemed spacious.

But Tuggle and Pierre brought jokes and fun into our lives. They were full of pranks that they played particularly on Gertie Kuzma and me. One day they caught a big snowshoe rabbit in one of their snares set around their shack on Martin Spit. After skinning the rabbit they carefully quartered it into sections as though it was a big game animal. When it had frozen overnight they took the carcass to Gertie and presented it as a frozen, dehydrated mountain sheep. Gertie was new to Alaska and was inclined to believe everything anyone told her. She marveled at the tiny, frozen, shrunken carcass until Tuggle's grin gave the joke away.

After a few of their tricks on me, I grew wary. One afternoon a coyote howl echoed from the ridge behind our cabin.

We rarely heard them howl in the daytime and it seemed too close to be natural, so I immediately suspected Tuggle was trying to scare me.

I'll fix him, I thought to myself. *He isn't going to sneak up on me.* Swiftly I mixed up a pot of cocoa and set the table with mugs and a plateful of cookies. Any minute I expected another howl as the Int-Hout boys reached the door.

The cocoa was ready and nothing happened. I waited, peeking out the door when 15 minutes had passed. A half-hour later I had to admit to myself they weren't coming and what I heard had really been a coyote howling in the woods. The Int-Hout boys had fooled me again.

MOST IMPORTANT to me, that winter I started to write. I had accumulated all kinds of "how to" books, and subscribed to the monthly *Writer* magazine. With no clear idea of how to go about it, I followed the advice Barrett Willoughby had given me some years before.

In the 1920s and 1930s Miss Willoughby had been a well-known writer whose books included *Spawn of the North, River House,* and *Alaska Holiday.* She had written an article about Ted, "Lighthouse Keeper at the End of the West," that was published in the *Saturday Evening Post.* They became friends, and Ted and I were married at her home on the San Francisco Peninsula.

"The way to learn to write is to write," she told me. "Do the best you can, and submit your work to the publishers. It will probably come back, but when you get to the point that you get criticism and suggestions on the rejection slips, you'll know you're making progress."

Another thing she told me was not to talk about my work. This was confirmed by things I read, and I found it to be valid advice. Ideas wear out if discussed. Stories must be thought out in secret, revised and refined, and not exposed prematurely. The satisfaction you get from telling your story will diminish the odds of ever writing it.

I started my book and no one knew anything about it, or even that I was writing.

THE COLD SPELL continued to the end of February. Frank Kuzma and Bill Eklof ran snarelines. They had great success catching coyotes and wolverines, but skinning was a problem. Their catch was usually frozen stiff by the time the snares were checked, and the carcasses were impossible to skin until thawed. Frank hung them in the cabin overnight, a messy, smelly procedure, and I was thankful Ted was not trapping.

He had done his share of trapping blue foxes and shooting brown bears when he was at the light station on Unimak Island in the Aleutians. When we first settled at Bear Cove his hunting instinct remained strong. Whenever a seal's sleek head popped out of the water, when a coyote or wolverine ran along the beach or crossed the ice on the frozen Cove, his first instinct was to shoot it.

As we became more attuned to our surroundings this killing instinct left him. He came to get more enjoyment out of watching animals than killing them, until in later years he no longer went hunting at all, except for ducks and geese at the head of the Bay. After our first year I never shot spruce chickens or rabbits, either. But like other homesteaders on the Kenai Peninsula, for a long time we depended on moose for our winter supply of meat.

After the first year Ted usually got a moose, not always in season but never more than one, which we shared with the neighbors. At first we tried to be legal about hunting, but after a few years we realized we could have less spoilage and make better use of the meat if we waited until freeze-up. I learned later that the Fish and Wildlife people were aware of what was going on but looked the other way as long as people didn't take meat to town, or shoot more game than they could use.

For a few years Ted hunted the meadows along upper Martin River and carried the meat over the ridge. This was a workout and had to be done in a hurry before the meat spoiled.

In later years he rowed the skiff past Martin River and into Battle Creek, to a slough by the old fox farm cabin, which was still in good shape, with bunks, kitchen stove and a cast-iron heater. He always made sure there was plenty of firewood in the woodshed, sometimes making a special non-hunting trip to replenish the fuel supply.

He rowed up on the tide the day before he intended to hunt, and stayed all night in the cabin. From its windows he could look over the Battle Creek flats, where almost always he got a moose as it fed early in the morning. Then he spent the day dressing out his kill, loaded it in the skiff and rowed home on the ebbing tide.

We had a good system for putting up moose meat and clams and salmon. We soon learned that quart jars were too large for the two of us and replaced them with wide-mouthed pint jars. We also invested in two 14-quart pressure cookers in which we could process 18 pint jars at a time.

Ted butchered the meat and cut it in chunks roughly two inches square. I packed the meat firmly into the jars and added a teaspoon of salt and sometimes a bay leaf or a clove of garlic. No water was added; the meat made its own juice that I later used for making gravy when serving the meat. We also boiled the bones for soup stock and processed it separately, adding dollops of marrow that Ted cracked and scraped out of the larger bones.

We filled the cookers with packed jars and processed according to cooker directions. While one cooker steamed we filled jars for the second one, which was ready to cook by the time the first one was taken off the stove. In two days we could process enough meat to last us the rest of the year.

While the other people at the Cove were enjoying themselves that cold winter, the new people at the fox farm were having problems. Looking after an unfamiliar place in a normal winter would have been hard enough. During the cold winter the problems were acute. Just keeping the uninsulated house warm was difficult, especially with the gigantic coal-eating kitchen range that no one but Harry Leonardt had ever been able to operate efficiently,

The plumbing froze. Their supplies grew short. First the Cove, then the entire Kachemak Bay froze completely. Tuggle and Pierre walked on the ice from the end of Martin River Spit in a straight line across Kachemak Bay to the mouth of McNeil Canyon. The *Nell* was frozen into the ice, and with no way to keep her pumped she was in danger of swamping. The ice surrounded the rotting pilings under the fox farm warehouse, and there was a possibility it might collapse.

One casualty of that cold winter was Lillian's lilac bush. The new people didn't wrap it in burlap as Harry had, and it was beaten by the icy winds. A hungry moose tore it apart and ate the smaller branches. By spring it was dead, and the gardens we had so admired vanished under the onslaught of weeds. The biggest of the new people's problems was that the woman was pregnant, the baby due in March. Gertie and I were horrified when we learned that the woman's plan was to stay at home, with Gertie and me to assist in the delivery. Gertie had two babies, but that didn't make her a midwife, and I had never given birth and had never even changed a baby's diaper.

Frank solved our dilemma. He hiked over the hill to the fox farm and assumed an oafish manner as he confronted the couple.

"Gertie and Elsa don't know nuthin' about birthin' babies. But I've delivered lots of calves. I'll help you all I can."

This prospect apparently changed the woman's mind. She left as soon as they could charter a plane from Homer to come and get her. Tuggle, Pierre and Frank helped drag a sled with her, her little girl and their luggage on it to Martin Spit where a ski plane could land on the beach above the broken shore ice. The weather broke before the plane returned for the luggage. It remained on the Spit until spring when the man from the fox farm picked it up by boat.

One night the last week in February, winter ended. When we went to bed the temperature was 35 degrees below zero. When we got up the next morning, it was 35 degrees above. A strong southeast wind had swept up from the Pacific, bringing warm weather with it.

Early spring at Bear Cove was like heaven. The sun climbed high in the sky instead of barely skimming above the mountains, so the country was bathed in glorious light. During the day it was warm enough to thaw, and bare patches appeared on south-facing slopes. The air itself was vibrant and lively.

In the woods the squirrels chattered at each other and fought great battles as mating season approached. The woodpeckers found long splinters on dead trees that acted as reeds and resonated all around the Cove when pounded by the strong-beaked birds.

In an attempt to make our cabin floor warmer, we had gathered dry grass in the clearing in fall and stuffed it as tightly as possible around the foundation pilings and under the bottom sill logs. During the winter a pair of minks had found this enclosed area, apparently liked it and moved in.

Every early morning we could hear the rustling of the dry grass as they pushed through it and settled down.

Since they hunted at night we never saw them. When warm weather came, however, they were disarmed of their caution. Now they emerged in the daytime, made a cozy bed in my flower garden beside the porch, and curled up in the sunshine. Our comings and goings did not disturb them as long as we did not move too quickly.

The ice that covered our part of the Cove almost every winter commenced to break up and went out in great pans on the big tides in March. Impatient to see the Cove clear of ice, we made an annual game of helping it along. Tidal action broke the shore ice in pieces, some small, others long and narrow. Sharp-pointed pike poles in hand, we scrambled across the broken ice to the end of Moose Point where the water was open, clear of ice.

Standing on the beach, or on the large unbroken pan of ice that covered most of the Cove surface, we speared into the broken pieces and pushed them toward open water. If the weather stayed mild we got rid of a lot of shore ice and had open water along the beach nearly to the warehouse.

We spent hours every spring wasting our energy on this useless work, but it seemed one of our rites of spring. A sudden cold snap could freeze all the water we had cleared, and once I fell in when my pike pole slipped and I lost balance. Ted was out of sight at the time, but I was able to swim through the pieces of broken ice and clamber up on the shore.

Springtime was also building time, and Ted's first project after the cabin was finished was to build a frame house he planned to join to the cabin's north wall. It was 12 x 18 feet, the same dimensions as the log cabin, and we planned to make it a bedroom and bathroom. As it turned out, Ted never finished it inside and we used it as a storeroom. He didn't like the appearance of the frame building adjoining the log cabin and also had trouble figuring out a way to join the two buildings, which were on slightly different levels. A few months later we moved the frame building to the other side and well away from the cabin.

THE SEASONS went by in an orderly pattern. Ted went to work in Seldovia in the middle of April and I remained at home. A few highlights distinguished the next few years, but essentially they were much the same. During the summer of 1947 I was completely alone at Bear Cove. The men were all fishing or employed by Seldovia canneries. This was about the time the Kuzmas came, but they had not yet arrived at the Cove. The Leonardts had moved to town and the new owners of the fox farm had not yet moved in.

Sometime in midsummer I noticed a haze hanging over the mountains and filling the hollows between the ridges. In the beginning I thought a volcano in the Aleutian Range was erupting and the prevailing southwest summer wind was driving the smoke toward the Kenai Peninsula.

Every morning the smoke grew thicker and lingered longer in the day. When I began to smell wood smoke I grew more alarmed. Every day I walked to the tip of Moose Point where I could look across Kachemak Bay to the Homer hills. Every day I expected to see the country in flames.

With no one to ask and no way to communicate with Seldovia or Homer, I could only worry. When I found out that the fire, burning thousands of acres farther north on the Peninsula, did not come within 60 miles of Bear Cove, I felt foolish for my unfounded fears.

The new people at the fox farm stayed one winter and summer and left the following autumn. This was a break for the Kuzmas, who were asked to live on the place as watch-men. The fox farm house was far more comfortable than the tiny Indian Island cabin; Gertie was happy to move. Frank Kuzma had homesteaded Bear Island across the Cove from the fox farm. He and Bill Eklof built a spacious log cabin the following winter, and another for Bill on his homesite across the Cove from us. I was pleased when the Kuzmas moved to the fox farm for that one year, for I could walk the beach to see Gertie without bothering Ted to take me through the woods.

Ted spent the larger part of a summer tearing down a cannery building at Tutka Bay. He came home with a scowload of beautiful lumber. We built a temporary dock to store the lumber, and Ted promised to build a house for us as soon as he found the proper site. The excess heavy lumber he sold provided the money to pay for our winter's grubstake.

My Private World

ALL DURING this time I worked on my book. As Barrett Willoughby had advised, I sent it to a publisher. It was rejected. I sent it out again and it came back, both times with printed rejection slips and no clue to what was wrong. When it came back the third time with no criticism or suggestions, I studied it with more critical eyes. It was no good, I admitted to myself, and I threw it out.

Not wanting to commit myself to another book-length project without really knowing what I was doing, I turned to short stories. The first to be accepted, in the summer of 1948, was "The Red Plane," published by *Alaska Life,* a magazine no longer in existence.

Encouraged, I wrote a six-part mystery serial that was

accepted by *Boys Today,* a weekly Sunday School magazine published by the Methodist Church. I found this market through *The Writer* magazine, which lists a variety of publications and their requirements in every monthly issue.

Ted had changed jobs and for a number of years ran a salmon cannery tender for the Seldovia Bay Packing Company and its successors. The job included bringing a boat from Seattle in the spring and returning it in autumn. This extended his absence from home to five months every year, but his steady earnings gave us the financial security we had been lacking in the first few years. As I started writing more and selling my work, I urged Ted to get started on his book. We had worked out a schedule so that even in a one-room cabin we had times of privacy. He got up around 5 a.m. and spent three hours drinking coffee and reading before I got up. On the other end of the day, he went to bed very early while I stayed up to read.

My writing time was during the day while he was occupied outdoors. Knowing he also dreamed of writing a book of Arctic adventure, I tried to persuade him to start. He needed more time to prepare, he told me. He would start writing when he was ready.

We still cleared land when weather permitted, but not with the sense of urgency of our first years on the homestead. We had applied for an extension on our land claim filing, and this had been granted since no one else was interested in homesteading in the area. Now our land clearing was focused on where we would find a place to build our house.

By this time chain saws were on the market and Ted bought one. When he brought it home, he proudly led me to a tree we had felled with the crosscut saw, to saw off a length and show me how well the saw would work. I was dazzled by the way the saw cut through the log and spit out a steady stream of small chips. Then it slowed, sputtered, and came to a halt.

"What's the matter?" I demanded. "Why did it stop?"

Ted tried to pull out the blade but it stuck tightly in the tree. He gave me a sheepish look.

"I must have been bending the saw."

I tried to hide my smile. I knew he was remembering, as I was, all those times he had yelled at me, "You're bending the saw!"

My sense of hope and contentment on the homestead received a jolt when Bill Eklof came home from fishing in 1950 and told me Ted had bought a fishing boat. I didn't believe him. Surely Ted would talk with me before he took such an important step. I usually went along with his plans, but I did want to be consulted.

A few days later Bill proved to be right. Ted came steaming into the Cove in a fishing boat he had agreed to take care of for the winter, with another boat in tow. This was the *Nancy-S.*, a 40-foot Army surplus J-boat that had been sold at a marshal's sale to a Seldovia fisherman, who then sold it to Ted. It looked like a wreck to me, but Ted was delighted with his "bargain." Our spare winter money had gone for the down payment. He had sent the diesel engine to Seattle for overhaul, and he planned to strip the boat house off, then rebuild it completely to his own liking

Inwardly, I was upset. How could he embark on such an investment without talking it over with me? Although I knew nothing about boats, I sensed that the payments and rebuilding costs would take more money than we could afford. Ted did not suspect my dismay, but I felt something serious had come between us. So far, our interests had been the same. When he bought the boat without discussing it with me, it was as though my opinions did not matter to him.

That was the start of my private world, a mental place where I could retreat and Ted had no part. So far his dreams had also been mine, but now this sense of unity began to fade. He later came to think I was afraid of the water, but it was the boat that I disliked.

Since he needed some kind of facility on the beach where he could work on the boat, Ted decided to build a warehouse with the lumber from Tutka Bay. I wasn't strong enough to help handle the heavy beams and timbers, so we hired a man from Seldovia, Johnny Kanaback, to come up for a couple of months to help Ted. While the men worked at building the warehouse, I kept house and had plenty of time to write.

My stories were mostly for young people, and almost everything I wrote was accepted by the first editor to whom it was submitted. I must have been one of a very few Alaska fiction writers during that time, and interest in the Territory seemed to be high. The Methodist publications were my main market but my work also was published by the Catholic, Baptist and Mormon magazines, as well as by *Children's Activities, The Alaska Sportsman,* and *Alaska Agriculturist* magazine.

People have asked me why I wrote for young people when I had no children of my own. My reasons were twofold. First, life in the wilderness seemed to lend itself to adventure stories most appealing to children. And second, I had a strong and vivid recollection of my own childhood and the stories I loved. From the time I first learned to read, I was a steady customer at the branch public library not far from my home. My childhood would have been dreary without those books, and I wanted to repay my pleasure to other children, by writing stories they would enjoy.

Ted and I had always expected to have a family, and our childlessness wasn't planned. I had inquired about correspondence courses for children and was prepared to raise our family in the wilderness. The opportunity did not material-ize. As it happened we were both members of families that were dying out. We both had brothers but they had no sons who married, so both family lineages are fading away.

DURING THIS period several unexpected events had sig-nificant effects on my future. First, we located one of Ted's half-brothers. Ted had no strong sense of family and made little effort to keep in touch with his relatives. He had only one sister, and the other children of his father had different mothers. Ted knew he had a half-brother, Walter, some-where in Alaska but made no effort to find him. We learned later that Walt had lived in Seldovia and Homer when we were already at Bear Cove, but somehow we had missed meeting him. By pure chance Ted eventually located him in Homer.

With Homer's dock periodically demolished by winter ice, and no sheltered place to anchor a boat, Kachemak Bay settlers found it more convenient to get mail and supplies in Seldovia even though it meant a longer boat trip. The new fox farm owner, however, did his business in Homer, and on one trip he asked Ted to go along. In the old Chamberlain and Watson store in Homer, Ted saw a business card stuck in the cash register, advertising Moose River Air Service oper-ated by Walt Pedersen.

Old Henry Chamberlain, who had known Ted's father in the Arctic, answered Ted's question. "Sure, that's your brother. He lives at Moose River."

We wrote to him, and during the following summer the two brothers met when Walt flew to Seldovia. A few days later Walt and his wife Laura came to see me at Bear Cove. We became friends. Over the years Walt and I carried on a correspondence, since neither Ted nor Laura was a letter writer. I visited Walt and Laura several times at Moose River, and Walt came to the Cove to dig clams and to visit us whenever he had business in the area.

Not long after the family connection was made, the men had a memorable hunting experience. Walt flew down from his Moose River homestead, and he and Ted left Bear Cove in the afternoon for a short flight to Bradley Lake in Walt's Champ, on floats, to check out the moose situation. It was the early September open season and Walt had been hunting the central part of the Kenai Peninsula with no luck.

On the river flats at the upper end of the lake they spotted a bull near a willow grove about a quarter-mile from the lake. They landed and set out on foot, splitting up to get the moose between them. Walt climbed a small hill overlooking the flats and could see Ted walking to the area where they had seen the moose. The bull stepped out in full view of Walt. He promptly fired a shot at it with his old 30-40 Krag that he'd carried in the airplane all summer as part of his emergency gear.

The bull took off running and Walt fired again. He could see the bullet splash in a pond about 20 feet back of the moose.

Just then Ted yelled, "You got him!" Walt shouted back, "No, he ran away!"

Ted hollered again, "He's lying in the willows, dead. I can see him."

Walt was more than a little confused—he had seen the bull vanish into the distance, unharmed.

He climbed down the hill to where Ted was and found him standing beside a very dead, and very illegal, cow moose. The cow had been well hidden in the willows, and Walt's first shot had killed her by accident, so to speak. They immediately set to work butchering and carrying meat down to the airplane. They had to hurry as dusk was starting to fall and Walt had to make several trips, flying the meat and Ted back to Bear Cove.

When Walt got back to his Moose River home he set up a target and found his rifle sights had gotten bent and the gun was shooting three feet to the left in a hundred feet. He had completely missed the bull and killed the cow he didn't even know was there. Many people do not believe the story to this day. Ted and I often laughed when we remembered Walt's rueful remark:

"This is a good hunting rifle when there are plenty of moose around."

During this time we got new neighbors when Ruth and Dana Newman moved down from Fairbanks to homestead the land adjoining ours. They also lived in tents for several years, and Ruth and I had an overland trail so we could visit each other whenever we wished, without being governed by the stage of the tide on the beach.

The fox farm changed hands again when Ben Culver, an Anchorage realtor, took over the place. He had big plans for an exclusive resort, and members of his family or hired caretakers lived on the place off and on for the next five or six years. With the Kuzmas on Bear Island, the Newmans adjoining us and Bill Eklof in his cabin across the Cove, we had more "nice neighbors" than I had expected in my most optimistic dreams.

More were to come. One summer day when I walked over to see Ruth and Dana Newman they had a visitor. His name was Gene, and he was scouting for homestead land for a group of would-be settlers. One of his group had known Ben Culver in California before World War II, and Ben had recommended Bear Cove. Gene had flown down to look over the area, and the Newmans had found him on the fox farm beach, with no one there and Gene not knowing where to look.

After we had considered and dismissed various places, I invited them to dinner and went home to cook and think some more. The group wanted five homesteads, and I knew from Ted's long search that such an amount of land was not available along the coast, particularly the potential agricultural land they had in mind. Then where would they find suitable land away from the shore?

Gradually my thoughts turned to the land bordering a small lake over the ridge, which we used to pass on hikes through the woods to visit Kuzmas when they lived in the cabin near Indian Island. The lake lay in the center of a wide flat area, heavily wooded for the most part, but also some grassland with a sunny exposure and a magnificent view of the mountains and glacier at the head of Martin River.

I made my suggestion while we were eating dinner. After we finished, since I did not trust myself to lead the way through the woods, we jumped into Dana Newman's skiff and buzzed out of the Cove and past Indian Island to the old log cabin. One of Paddy's hunting and trapping trails led inland, and when it forked with one branch going over the hill to the fox farm, we took the other that led to the lake.

When we reached the lakeshore opening we stopped and gazed in silence. The sun had set but still glowed against the snow-capped peaks and the glacier in the distance. The lake lay as silver as an old mirror, and on the opposite shore a moose, half hidden in the tall grass, studied us across the water.

Though he didn't say much, Gene decided he had found their land. He left the next day to lead the group to their new home.

In amazement I watched the arrival of the Pomeroy group. They seemed to have everything. The gravel bar that surrounded the little log cabin where the Kuzmas had lived was crowded with homestead gear of every description. Several tents were packed with tools and equipment. They had a dismantled sawmill, building materials, many cases of groceries, farming equipment, even a Jeep and another one parked on Homer Spit along with a moving van.

To my bedazzled eyes, the people were equally exotic. The group had been formed in Vienna, Austria, where they had worked together in the Allied military government set up after World War II. Before the war Harold Pomeroy had been a political figure in California, where he had known Ben Culver. Gene and his wife, Daphne, both had been in the armed forces, while Roxolana Skobelska was a displaced person from the Ukraine who had worked as an interpreter for the Allies in Vienna after fleeing the Russians with her parents. Along the way the group had picked up a serviceman, Al, a brawny young man who was as out of place as a rooster in a flock of peacocks.

Gene and Daphne bought the log cabin from a Seldovia fisherman and staked a 160-acre homestead around it. Because of their military service they did not have to clear and cultivate any land in order to prove up. The others chose acreage inland surrounding the little lake.

Daphne became the cook for the group, while the others set out to build a road to the lake. They soon discovered, as we had earlier, that one thing they needed and lacked was a bulldozer. I had never in my life seen people work so hard. With axes, picks, crowbars, mattocks and shovels they grubbed out stumps, rocks, and rotted moss-buried tree trunks. It took them most of the summer to make a road that was passable to the lake with the Jeep.

Young Al left, worn out and seeing no future for himself with the group. Harold Pomeroy, nicknamed Pom, built a log cabin near the lake that was part of his homestead. They started to clear land and dreamed of the greenhouses they would build to embark on hydroponic farming.

That winter was a time of sociability around the Cove. Every week invitations were exchanged, so we often had guests or were invited somewhere. We hiked overland to Newmans' and over the ridge, but to visit Kuzmas we went in the skiff.

Coming home over the water from those visits was chilly and slow, but also interesting. The wintry nights were cold and clear, the air completely clean and unpolluted. Our view of the sky was awesome: brilliant stars, constellations and planets. No wonder, I thought, that people from the most primitive times saw signs and symbols in the stars.

The winter sea also offered mystery. We experienced the "fire in the water" observed by fishermen the world over. Behind us as we rowed we could see our trail in the water, the cold fire of phosphorescence marking the path of the skiff, and every oar stroke like stitches in the water.

We would stop and drift, beaming our flashlight down, to see the myriad of life forms drawn to the light. Shrimp of all sizes were particularly active and made us laugh with their sidewise swimming movements.

Sometimes when we dug clams at night we saw the beady reflective eyes and shadowy outlines of hundreds of spider crabs drawn to the shallows by the light of our lantern.

MY FATHER sent me money for a trip back home, so I spent a winter Outside. Ted remained at the Cove and started to build a lean-to onto the cabin. He decided this addition would look better than attaching the frame building to one end, and would provide us with a bedroom and pantry which we needed badly. Five months in Utah and California were enough to convince me that my future lay in

Alaska. My family ties were weakened and I had lost track of most of my friends. Those who remained regarded me as an entertaining novelty, and they wanted to hear only the most hair-raising accounts of my experiences. Over the ensuing years I have kept in touch with only one of my girlhood friends, who is still dearer than a sister to me.

One thing that surprised me was to discover how much I had developed physically during the years on the homestead. All that sawing, chopping and turning the winch handle had developed my shoulders so that the sleeves of an old jacket left behind now ended halfway up my arms. My muscles matched my height. Once, when he did not realize I could hear him, Kinky Alexander had remarked, "My God, she's a husky woman."

By April I was ready to go home to Alaska. Ted had already started work for the summer and we met briefly in Seattle. I hoped he would tell me he had started to write his book but the subject was not mentioned. He was busy with the loading of the cannery tender he was to take North, and I sensed that I was in his way. I was glad when the steamship *Denali* sailed and I embarked on my last voyage by ship between Seattle and Seldovia.

EIGHT

Wilderness
Takes Its Toll

AFTER THE excitements of traveling and visiting, it was good to get back to Bear Cove and to live alone for a while. Ted had put in the foundation, floor and two or three log rounds of the cabin lean-to. Since this made our old door in the rear of the cabin inaccessible to the outdoors, he had cut a new door in the south end of the cabin and built a sturdy porch. This was the sunny end and made the entrance more pleasant, especially in winter, and I liked it.

I lost my friend Gertie Kuzma that winter while I was away. She had suffered a nervous breakdown and was taken to Seattle for shock treatments.

Although we had often visited, Gertie had never confided her worries and fears to me. Her husband and children meant everything to her, and if she was not completely enthusiastic about their move to Alaska, she felt she had no choice. Frank's mind was made up and she came along with him. She spoke often of her sisters and Frank's relatives whom she seemed to miss, but from his remarks it appeared Frank did not share her strong sense of family. He was happy trapping and building, and fishing commercially in the summers.

For some women, living in wilderness Alaska was a matter of quiet endurance. Gertie adapted as best she could. She was a wonderful cook and we looked forward to her dinner invitations. She had complete control of her wood and coal kitchen range and made dainties as delicate as Boston cream pies and creampuffs. Her house was immaculate and her little girls always neat and clean. She did not read much for pleasure or do any kind of fancywork. Her husband's and children's welfare was her only interest.

No one realized the depth of her mental distress. She was afraid of the water but Frank chose to settle on an island. Her sister came on a visit from Michigan but did not like Alaska and did not stay very long. This was a great disappointment to Gertie. Her oldest daughter was ready for school, but Gertie did not feel capable of teaching her.

When the breakdown came, it was complete. After the treatments in Seattle Frank brought her home, but she soon started to regress. At the end of summer when Frank came back from the fishing grounds, they sold out and went back to Michigan, where she eventually recovered.

The Kuzmas were not the only neighbors we lost that year. Tuggle and Pierre were tired of their rootless lives in the wilderness, and after the commercial salmon fishing season they settled down in Seldovia.

Frictions soon developed among the Pomeroy group. Gene and Daphne wanted out but needed traveling money and had no way to withdraw their investment since it had all been spent on supplies, tools and equipment. They spent the summer in Seldovia, where she worked in the cannery while he was Ted's deckhand on a cannery tender. At the end of the season they headed down the highway in the Jeep that was part of their settlement from the homesteading venture.

Two other partners had invested in the enterprise. For one reason or another neither of them came to take out land at Bear Cove.

Pom's son Rodney came up from California and with his wife, Carol, and their small son joined the homesteading group across the ridge. They set up the sawmill and sawed lumber to build a house for themselves. Pom's wife, who had remained in Vienna until the group got settled, changed her mind about moving North. They divorced, and Pom and Roxy subsequently married.

With all these comings and goings, Bear Cove was a living soap opera, although that term was not known to me at the time. I remained an observer; we tried not to take sides in other people's problems, but I was fascinated and tried to keep informed on what was happening.

We had a good trail, and later a road, over the hill to the Pomeroy settlement. Now that I no longer needed to fear getting lost, I enjoyed the hike through the woods. There was no place on the trail where an animal could be cornered or trapped so that it might charge at me. I had learned from observation that most wild creatures were terrified of humans, anyway, and would run away faster than I could. If I met a bear or a moose in the woods, I was confident it would crash through the trees and brush on either side of the trail. In Southeast Alaska I had heard it said that while 24 bears might be harmless, the next one could be a dangerous rogue. Luckily for me, I never met that 25th bear.

At about the time new people moved into the Kuzma place on Bear Island, Ruth and Dana Newman moved to

Homer. Their place was bought by an officer from Elmendorf Air Force Base near Anchorage who spent only one vacation at the Cove. His wife was a city person, so fearful of the wilderness she wouldn't go to the outhouse by herself. Their place remained vacant for many years, then was bought as a vacation spot by a car dealer in Soldotna.

The fox farm was inhabited intermittently, by the Culver family or by watchmen they hired. Ben Culver still had dreams of converting the place into an exclusive wilderness lodge. He formed a partnership with a carpenter with whom we became friends. The man did a lot of work on the white cottage, raising the roof and adding a full second floor in place of the long narrow attic. He also put in the foundation and part of the framing for a large addition that was to be the main part of the lodge.

The partnership fell apart. The carpenter left and was replaced by a watchman and his family, who stayed for several years. One good thing for all of us was that Ben Culver had installed a short-wave radio to communicate with Homer and beyond. The watchman was generous about sending and relaying messages for us, so we were no longer completely isolated.

My sister Edith came to spend the summer of 1951 with me, while her husband worked on a cannery tender. We had a fine time together, boating, digging clams, and visiting over the hill occasionally. Ruth Thomas, on the island at the Kuzma place, was alone. Her husband had gone fishing with Bill Eklof. Edith and I rowed over to see her once or twice a week, and we went to various beaches around the Cove for picnics. Although I did not know it then, this was to be the last summer I spent in the Cove for many years.

FOR A number of years, while we slowly paid for the hull, Ted's boat lay in Bear Cove at anchor. He had stripped off the cabin and covered the opening with canvas. I kept it pumped out in the summer, rowing out and climbing aboard once or twice a week. The hull leaked a little and it was a chore to pump it—more so in winter. Since the inner Cove iced up every year, in late autumn Ted moved the boat between two islands near the mouth of the Cove where Kachemak Bay swells kept the water from freezing. This meant keeping a skiff on a beach near the boat, so he could walk overland and then row out to the boat to pump it.

As time went on, the boat changed our lives completely. Ted forgot his dream of buying a sawmill. He gave up the idea of raising cattle once our land was cleared and cultivated. The boat, and the king crabs and salmon we caught in the Cove, made him decide to build and operate a small cannery. We had home-packed the fish and colorful red king crab legs in our pint glass jars. Ted was sure we could make our living producing a similar pack commercially.

He filed on a Trade and Manufacturing Site at the head of Bear Cove, where a stream tumbled down a steep canyon from the lake above. We cleared the land and for a while Ted wanted to sell the homestead and move to what we called the cannery site. He had plans to raise the water level of the lake that fed the stream, build a flume and install a Pelton wheel so we could have electricity.

While I went along with the cannery plan, I disagreed about moving to the cannery site. It was a small shelf against the steep hill, with mountains behind that cut off the sun for the five winter months. Realizing how much we appreciated the sun on our cabin, I knew I could not live in shadows for almost half of every year. While Ted could talk confidently about making a flume by tunneling 50 feet through solid rock so we could have electricity, I was unwilling to make another move and start all over again.

It bothered me too that the head of the Cove was frozen

solid every winter from late December until the end of March. The same situation locked up our homestead, but we could reach open water by walking a quarter-mile through the woods to Newmans' old place, which was on the open-water side of Moose Point. To walk there from the cannery site would be an additional hike of more than a mile.

Ted had far more imagination and confidence than I. Reared in a family where money was always limited and my parents were harassed by debts, I worried about our future. Now that Ted had invested in the boat I felt we should pay for it and get it in operation before we started some other enterprise.

I still longed for a more comfortable home, while Ted spent his energy remodeling the cabin. Over the years he moved the door from the side to one end and then the other, rearranged the lean-to several times by cutting in a new door and closing the original one, making a partition between bedroom and pantry and tearing it out, then removing the whole wall between lean-to and front room and replacing it with plywood. He cut new windows in both cabin end walls, and finally cut out all the front and side log walls and re-placed them with timbers and plywood, so the top logs, gables and rafters remained the only evidence of the old log cabin. All this time he planned to build a new house for us when he could find exactly the right spot.

As my dreams evaporated in the face of reality, over the hill the Pomeroy families also had disappointments. They had hired a tractor and its operator to come in to clear a field for potatoes and other root vegetables. In addition they had a large area smoothed and graded for the two greenhouses they built. These structures were each approximately a hundred feet long and 40 feet wide, with frames of wood covered with heavy plastic sheathing. Inside, they constructed a large system of troughs for hydroponic gardening. Both buildings were heated by woodstoves, which meant an endless job of cutting firewood, and someone to sleep in the greenhouse at night to keep the fires going.

They raised the most beautiful tomatoes and cucumbers I had ever seen, on vines that climbed into the tops of the buildings. But they soon learned that it was not production but marketing that was their fatal problem. With no road to Homer, the crop had to be transported by plane or boat, neither of which they had.

The main marketing advantage of their crops was that they were vine-ripened. This meant the produce should be picked as it ripened and taken to town daily, but this proved to be ruinously expensive. In addition, Homer could not absorb their production, which meant shipping to Anchorage and Kodiak. There, stores would not contract for less than all-year production, since if they bought Alaska products in summer, Seattle wholesalers would not ship to them in winter. One more Alaska dream was shattered.

Growing potatoes turned out to be the same story. They built a gigantic, cavern-sized storage cellar and planted a field of potatoes, cabbage and other crops. They had more success disposing of them but still had competition from every would-be farmer from Homer to Sterling. The young Pomeroys went back to California, and Pom and Roxy turned to logging and cutting lumber for their livelihood.

Meanwhile, my thoughts were dismal. I considered all the people who had come and gone from the area—the Leonardts, Culvers, Kuzmas and the Int-Hout brothers, the Newmans, Thomases, the Magees of Aurora Lagoon, and most of the Pomeroy group. I thought of all the wilderness women I knew or had heard of who had become "odd" as a result of their lonely lives. Some harbored delusions, two became alcoholics, and one committed suicide. In my lowest moments I wondered which course I would take.

I was bothered also by our hand-to-mouth life, when we should have been making tangible progress to provide a secure future. I was nearly 40 and Ted approaching 50. We hadn't saved a cent, were in debt, and used up Ted's earnings as soon as they came in.

I decided to go to work. I told Ted that I was tired of spending the summers alone and wanted to get out among more people. The cannery superintendent had already offered me an office job when I met him in Seattle on my trip two years before. When I wrote saying I was available, he hired me immediately.

Summers in Seldovia

AFTER THE placid, uneventful life in Bear Cove, Seldovia was exciting and interesting. This cannery town, near the mouth of Cook Inlet, is separated from the rest of the Kenai Peninsula by Kachemak Bay and the rugged peaks and glaciers of the Kenai Mountains.

When I started to work there, the town was a seasonal community that fell dormant at the end of the salmon fishing season. Then all the cannery people and many of the fishermen and their families left Alaska, with only a few year-round residents content to spend an inactive and quiet winter.

Seldovia had been a Russian trading post before Alaska was purchased by the United States in 1867. There is no written pre-American history, but apparently the village grew up around the Russian store and was not an ancient Native village as was English Bay.

Many of the old Seldovia families are descendants of Russian Church functionaries, or men who came from the other states and Scandinavian countries to participate in the early herring, cod and salmon fisheries. Some of these men married Kenai Peninsula or Susitna Indian women and settled in the village. Their names are still carried by many Seldovia people—Colberg, Ollestad, Elvsaas, Josefsen and Saracof, Balashof and Kashevarof, among others.

At the time I began working there, four salmon canneries operated in Seldovia, in addition to a cold storage plant that processed halibut and a reduction plant that converted cannery waste to fish meal to be processed into animal feed.

"My" cannery, Seldovia Bay Packing Company, was in the heart of town, where the road to the airfield and the power plant met the boardwalk. The cold storage and reduction plants had connections with our cannery, physically as well as financially, and their employees slept in the same bunkhouse and ate in the common mess hall.

I finally met the wives and families of men who had come up the bay to hunt and fish and had anchored at our homestead to visit and have a meal. These were for the most part year-round Seldovia residents, which gave me contacts other than fellow cannery workers, who seemed to be totally immersed in their jobs. The seasonal workers didn't listen to news broadcasts or have other contacts with the outside world; they were obsessed with processing salmon.

My job was exciting except for the first summer, when I was buried in the commissary office as the bookkeeper, with little or no contact with the public. One friend I made was Esther Int-Hout, the bride of Tuggle, who had come from Illinois a few months before I moved to town. She also worked in the commissary, and we have remained friends over the years. I also got to know other cannery workers and began to learn the fishing industry.

One good thing about working in the commissary was that we had regular hours and did not have to go back to work after supper even when the cannery operated overtime.

Esther, Bertha Krueth and I often cooked supper together at Esther's or Bertha's house. Their husbands were fishermen so they were alone, and I was glad to get away from the mess hall occasionally. We always had plenty to talk about, discussing our fellow employees and the fishermen. Our gossip sessions were a welcome relief from the insular atmosphere of the cannery.

The next year I was transferred to the cannery office at one end of the mess hall adjoining the boardwalk, where all the activities of the town passed before my eyes. The air taxi operator who carried freight and passengers between Seldovia and Homer brought his Jeep to the boardwalk in front of our office door. We served as an unofficial office for him until he set up his own place of business, so we saw almost everybody who came to and left town.

I got along well with Harry Tallman, a former Navy officer and graduate of Annapolis who was the cannery superintendent, and with Sam Rubinstein, who took over ownership of the company the year I started to work in the main office. The atmosphere was friendly and informal, particularly early in the season when the pressures of processing and competition with the other plants had not yet started.

As assistant bookkeeper I did all the posting of fishermen and payroll accounts, so I knew how many fish everyone was catching and how many hours people worked. Since one of my jobs was to handle fishermen's mail, I also kept track of where they fished and the routes of the cannery tender that picked up the fish. In this way I got to know most of the people Ted had told me about, since we worked for the same company.

Luckily for me, Olaf Floe, the head bookkeeper, had had years of experience in cannery work and taught me the fundamentals of the fish business. We worked together in harmony and respect and are still friends more than 30 years after we started to work together.

While interesting, the work was arduous. My day started at 6:45, when the superintendent had his first radio schedule with the tenders on the fishing grounds. They reported the number of fish already picked up, told of any boat trouble they might be having, and relayed orders for groceries they wanted sent out by the next tender. My job was to take down the orders and messages in shorthand, transcribe them and turn them over to the commissary or others to whom they were directed. The orders would be ready for tender pick-up for the return trip as soon as the fish were unloaded.

Breakfast was at 7:30, announced by the howl of a horn that could be heard all over the cannery complex. Sixty people were served, the administrative staff at the head table, the machinists, beach gang, cold storage and reduction plant workers at another, and the Filipino crew at the third, at the end nearest the stove and the clean-up area. Our cannery did not have a "Blue Room," a separate dining room for executives where the meals might be more elaborate than those served the rest of the crew. This had been general cannery practice in earlier times and was still practiced in some canneries in more isolated areas.

Meals were not social occasions, except when we had interesting visitors. Usually everyone ate fast and in silence, then left to relax outdoors or in the bunkhouse until work started again.

The local employees, mostly women who lived at home, were on call and did not eat in the mess hall. There was a small bunkhouse available for women who came from out of town, but they did their own cooking and housekeeping. In such a small community everyone knew the probable time the cannery would operate, and a warning whistle shrilled over the harbor one hour before ring-in time.

If an unexpected load of fish arrived, one of my jobs was to make the rounds of the town to call out the workers. The cannery owned a bicycle that I used to get around town and to take and pick up mail from the post office. On the steeper back roads it was easier to walk, and I got plenty of exercise. I knew where everyone lived or where they might be if they were not at home when I called for them. There were no residential telephones, only one line to Homer that was installed in a private dwelling and was used as a pay phone by all who needed it. Adam Lipke maintained a wireless station with contacts to Anchorage and Outside.

Early in the summer the pace was leisurely and our work was light. I had time after work to visit with the friends I made, as long as I reported for the last radio schedule of the day, at 8:15 p.m.

Gradually, as the salmon came into Cook Inlet, the pace of Seldovia life quickened. The fishermen who had gone to Cordova for the early Copper River run returned to fish in Cook Inlet. Boats also came from Kodiak, and our roster of fishermen grew. The setnetters who fished along the beaches on either side of Cook Inlet and on Kalgin Island started earlier than the boats, hoping to catch the diminishing run of king (chinook) salmon.

The Fourth of July marked the real start of the red (sockeye) salmon run. Seldovia was noted for its Independence Day celebration, which was also a send-off for the fishing fleet. The townspeople traditionally went all-out to provide games and races for the children, a parade along the boardwalk of floats built on cannery hand trucks, and contests and races for the men and a few uninhibited young women. Booths were set up by various organizations, to sell hot dogs, soft drinks, popcorn and souvenirs.

The men's tug-of-war sometimes developed into a grudge fight, Seldovia fishermen on one end of the rope and outsiders on the other. The game usually ended with a tremendous surge, one side ignominiously dragged by the other along the graveled road outside the cannery office. Then most of the contestants adjourned to the taverns, where arguments sometimes turned into terrible fistfights that raged up and down the boardwalk.

Since my room was over the office on one end of the bunkhouse, I had a grandstand seat to the bloody carnage that ended when Dick Miller, the town policeman, waded in and ended the fights by dragging the contestants off to jail.

Three taverns and two package stores served Seldovia's alcohol appetite. The Polar Bar was operated by Joe Hill, the town's only black man, who was known as "the whitest man in Seldovia." His bar was situated at one end of town not far from the Morris and Morris grocery store. The Surf Club and the Linwood Bar and Cafe were neighbors in the center of town, not far from the Seldovia Bay Packing Company cannery. The Seldovia House, the only hotel, was directly across the road from the Linwood. With the movie house operating only intermittently, the taverns were the main place of entertainment. A Pentecostal church had a resident minister, while a Catholic priest and a Methodist minister came occasionally from Seward or Homer to conduct services.

When full boatloads of salmon started coming in, no one had much time or energy for evening entertainment. All the canneries operated at full capacity. The cans were shipped from Seattle without ends, the bodies pushed flat. The can re-form lines pounded and jangled as the can bodies were punched round and bottoms clinched-on and the cans then danced down a conveyor to the filler. The Filipinos had started work earlier, pushing salmon into the "Iron Chink," a massive water-spraying, many-bladed machine that de-headed and de-tailed the fish and removed most of the guts. This machine replaced the hand work of Chinese contract laborers who had been employed during the early days of salmon canning.

The fish were sluiced down a trough to the sliming table, where women in raingear trimmed off the remaining entrails and fins, scraped off the slime and blood under taps of running water and sent the cleaned fish down the line to the cutter. This wicked-looking machine, with rotating blades set apart the height of a can of salmon, was also operated by Filipinos, who were the most skilled and experienced of the cannery workers.

The woman who operated the filler was regarded as one of the most important of the local workers. Her keen eyes judged the weight of the fish to exactly fill a one-pound can. A dollop of salt was added automatically, then the cans, moving upright along the line, were automatically weighed and any too light or too full were diverted to the patching table. A woman on either side of that line adjusted the contents to proper weight, using snippets of fish brought to her in trays, and re-weighed each rejected can before replacing it on the processing line.

The throb of the vacuum pump was the pulse of the cannery, each beat registering the passage of a can of salmon. Lids were clamped on automatically and the filled cans tumbled into the retort tray. All cannery operations had to be co-ordinated, and a jam or breakdown anywhere along the line meant stopping the entire production.

These stoppages, if longer than a few minutes, were a signal for the workers to go out into the sunshine and perch along the boardwalk or dock railings to enjoy an unexpected rest. Regularly there was a rest break every two hours, a mug-up time when coffee and cookies were put out for the workers on their 15-minute recess. On days when the work was unusually hard or the hours stretched into overtime, the head cook, Max Benito, made an extra effort with the mug-up goodies, baking cinnamon rolls, sheet cakes or nut-filled brownies.

At the end of the production line, stacks of metal trays, each holding 12 dozen cans of salmon, were piled on a dolly that ran along tracks leading into the retorts. These long round chambers were oversized pressure cookers where the filled cans were processed.

The "fish cook" also had an important job, keeping the steam at its correct pressure, regulating the oil furnace and boiler that made the steam, and keeping track of processing time for each retort. Sometimes I would see him hanging out the window that overlooked the boardwalk, taking a few minutes to grab some fresh, cool air away from the steamy retort area.

When the cans of fish were cooked and the steam bled off, the retorts were flushed with cold water before they were opened. Then the racks were wheeled into the warehouse for cooling overnight. Early the next morning before the cannery line started to operate, the cans were boxed into 48-can cases by the Filipino crew, who counted on this overtime to increase their season's earnings.

About once a month an Alaska Steamship Company freighter came into the port to pick up the salmon pack and frozen halibut. Sometimes there were arguments among plant operators about who would get most of the shipping space. If last year's pack had been sold out at its destination, early shippers had a distinct market advantage.

Head bookkeeper Olaf Floe was a feisty man. He once delayed a freighter from departing when he and the ship's first mate, who had spent several hours in one of the local taverns, couldn't agree on the case count of our shipment. Olaf typed a note on the bill of lading to the effect that the mate was drunk, and refused to remove it when requested to do so by our superintendent and the ship's captain. I felt bad when, after an hour's futile argument, Harry Tallman ordered me to retype the shipping papers without Olaf's memo, and the superintendent signed them.

I found my job stimulating and always enjoyed being sent on errands out of the office. When the cannery was operating I liked to go through the large front door and to feel I was part of it all. In the warehouse the crew might be stacking cases ready to ship, with the forklift truck moving between the stacks and the upright building timber supports. Or trays with hot, filled cans might be wheeled from the retorts on hand trucks, with the Filipinos shouting warning cries.

Bedlam seemed to reign in the canning wing, where machinery throbbed, the processing line rattled and jangled, water was apt to spray unexpectedly, and men occasionally whistled at me playfully from the shadows. Although small frictions sometimes cropped up, on the whole the crew worked well together. Many of the machinists, beach gang, Filipinos and women workers returned year after year and knew each other well.

The cannery had been built and added to over the years, so it contained many odd-shaped rooms and crannies. The original building was a large log cabin, later expanded in all directions. To me this added to its charm and mystery, although in truth it made for an inefficient operation.

With both of us working, Ted and I were doing better financially, and he ordered materials to rebuild his boat. He had a Seattle marine architect draw up plans for the conversion and ordered the materials through the cannery. He was an excellent tender operator, hard-working, completely honest and expert at spotting schools of fish for the fishermen. This gave the plant operators confidence in him and he was extended unlimited credit. I was appalled at the way the bills piled up, but Ted was undismayed, remaining cheerful and confident.

The boat hull had previously undiscovered flaws, and Ted had to replace the bowstem and some of the timbers and planks. Taking pride in his work and demanding perfection of himself, he made the repairs, working at home after the fishing season and in early spring. Since we had no electricity he had to use hand tools and it all took a lot longer than he had expected.

When the Cove iced up and he couldn't work on the boat on the beach, we went back to clearing land. While we had given up plans to farm or raise cattle, we still had to clear and cultivate 10 acres to "prove up" on our claim in order to receive title to the 80 acres upon which we had filed.

During this period I was writing whenever I could but was not accomplishing very much. In the summer there was no time, and in winter I was on call to help Ted, and my mind was in a turmoil. For Ted, writing was out of the question and the only time he talked about it was when someone came to visit and he revealed his dreams.

Across the ridge the people were struggling to make a living. To me, it seemed a tragic waste of brains and energy to see two people work so hard to wrest a living from the land. We all seemed to be fighting a losing battle, but no one would admit it.

From my visits with Ted's brother Walt and his wife Laura in Sterling, I had already concluded that there were two types of homesteaders. One group came to Alaska as the settlers had gone into the uncivilized American West, to make their homes and fortunes in a place that would eventually develop into a settled part of the country. The like-minded Alaska homesteaders settled along the Sterling Highway right-of-way, or near existing settlements that would be connected to the area road and school systems some day.

The other kind of homesteaders were those who wanted to get away from civilization and not be drawn into it later. They staked their homesteads mainly to protect themselves from people who otherwise might settle too close. Some of these would-be hermits chose sites on the lakes beyond the mountains on the west side of Cook Inlet, and on the south side of Kachemak Bay where because of the mountains and glaciers there could never be a connecting road and access would remain by boat or plane.

Ted and I fitted into this category, and I began to see we would never have permanent neighbors, only enthusiastic newcomers who would soon leave in disappointment when they could find no way of making a living. This had already happened many times, and the upper Kachemak Bay shore-line was dotted with abandoned places of settlement.

For a number of years we and the Pomeroys were the only people at Bear Cove during the winter. We all worked hard on our own pursuits and saw each other mainly on mail days. Our visits were happy and cheerful, a pleasant change from the daily grind.

We also spent most of the holidays together, at our place or theirs. Christmas was the big day of the year and we cel-ebrated twice. Roxy's background was Greek Catholic, and they celebrated on the Slavic date which, like Russian Christmas celebrated by Alaska Natives, fell 12 days later than the date of the holiday marked by most European and western hemisphere countries. Roxy's mother lived in New York and sent her Ukrainian dainties and recipes for tradi-tional food which Roxy did her best to prepare.

I also developed certain traditions which we followed over the years. Our cabin was too small for a Christmas tree, so I fastened spruce boughs over and around the windows and festooned them with the few ornaments we had, including gilded nuts and animal crackers, which my family had used as tree ornaments when I was a child.

We had a turkey and a bottle of Demerara rum brought up on the mail plane, and with the treats sent to us by relatives and friends as well as goodies I concocted, we usually had a cheerful holiday season.

TEN

'Victory at Bear Cove'

THE YEAR I turned 40, 1955, was a watershed year for me. This came about through an accident in the cannery. Six or seven cardboard salmon cases filled with old financial records were stacked in one corner of the office. I needed information from one of the boxes, and with no one around to help me, I tugged on the topmost case and the whole stack leaned toward me. In my effort to keep it from collapsing I clung to the case, and its momentum as it fell twisted me around and threw me to the floor.

After a few days of agony, with pains in my back and down my leg, with toes numb and one foot out of control, the local doctor sent me to Anchorage to an orthopedic surgeon. The upshot was surgery to remove an extruded disc, three weeks in the hospital, and a heavy metal, leather and felt brace from my shoulders to my waist.

I finished out the summer in the cannery office, working on a limited basis. Back at Bear Cove in the fall, my entire homestead life changed. It was hard for me to lift my feet so I had trouble walking on uneven ground. No longer could I work in the woods, carry buckets of water and coal, or wash on a washboard. Part of my earnings went for a gasoline-powered washing machine, and Ted took over all the other chores I had done. I stayed near the house all winter, too fearful of falling to attempt to rove out of the clearing.

No one lived at the fox farm, the Newman place was deserted, and Bill Eklof had abandoned his place as too lonely and moved to Peterson Bay, closer to Homer and Seldovia. The Bear Island place was vacant. Roxy was still on the homestead across the ridge, but Harold Pomeroy took a job in Juneau and was gone much of the time, finally conceding it was impossible to make a living in the wilderness.

The only people who had ever made a living off the land in upper Kachemak Bay were the fox farmers in the 10 or 15 years following the First World War. In that era there were thriving fox farms at Aurora Lagoon, Bear Cove, Battle Creek and Bradley River. Now all these places were vacant and deteriorating, and all the fox farmers were dead. Harry Leonardt had continued to insist that cigarettes wouldn't hurt him as long as he rolled his own. He died in Seldovia one morning in a coughing fit, over his first cup of coffee and a cigarette.

Hilmer Olsen of Bradley River, our first upper-bay friend after he had moved to Seldovia and before we moved to Bear Cove, came to an even more tragic end. His wife grew senile, and her son made arrangements for her to enter a nursing home and for Hilmer to go to the Pioneer Home at Sitka. He was nearly blind and would soon be helpless to care for himself. One day he put his old squirrel-shooting rifle to his head and pulled the trigger. His neighbor found Hilmer in his woodshed the next morning, still sitting upright, his life ebbed. All these things were on my mind that winter when I was housebound. I was accustomed to an active and vigorous outdoor life, but gradually I saw the blessing in disguise. At last I had plenty of time to write, and I would never have to work in the woods again.

Since leaving California I had kept in touch with my mentor, Barrett Willoughby. She was pleased with the progress I had made and always encouraged me. When I visited her on my trip Outside, she was concerned about Ted when I told her he was still "getting ready" to write his book.

"Make him start," she told me. "I know a man 90 years old who is still getting ready. Tell Ted to quit talking and start writing."

The subject was so ticklish that I did not deliver her message. In every letter Barrett nagged at him until it became a sore point. Finally, in the winter I was disabled I asked her in a letter not to mention the subject again.

That winter was the start of my first serious writing efforts. By spring I had written another six-part serial and several short stories that were all accepted by various youth magazines. And I had started thinking about trying another book.

I had to wear the back brace a second year, but that did not stop me from working in Seldovia the next summer. Ted also still worked for the cannery, running one of the big tenders. He grew weary of the long runs and constant problems with crew and beach gang and asked to be transferred to a smaller tender that remained on the fishing grounds all season. He worked more closely with the fishermen, relieving them of their catch so they wouldn't overload, and handling their supplies and mail.

Most of all, he enjoyed cruising the fishing grounds before the fishing periods opened, trying to locate the schools of salmon and alert "his" fishermen. His little tender, the *Iron Mule,* was a surplus Navy power scow and required only a two-man crew, which suited Ted.

Our account at the cannery was growing astronomically as Ted still ordered material and equipment for his boat. I overheard grumblings between the superintendent and the cannery owner, and could see by Ted's progress on the boat rebuilding that his own fishing days were not yet in sight.

"You've got to do something," I cried in anguish at the end of the 1956 season, when the subject of money came up. "We're not making any progress. We're going under."

"I've been thinking about that," he replied slowly.

This was the first indication of any concern on his part. We had never sat down and really discussed financing of the boat and making plans for the future. For 15 years our lives had been guided by our whims and impulses, most of which had not worked out. Now, for the first time, Ted proposed a practical solution.

Some time earlier he had met an old acquaintance on the Seldovia dock. Nils Thomsen had been a crewman on the lighthouse tender *Cedar* when Ted was also in the Lighthouse Service. Now Thomsen owned the small ship *Expansion* that carried mail and supplies between Seward and the Aleutian Islands. He had offered Ted a job which Ted declined at the time. With our fortunes at their lowest ebb, Ted wrote to Nils and asked for a job. The answer soon came. He should be in Seward in time to make the January 1957 mail run to the Aleutians.

I was to stay home alone, partly for the classic homesteader's reason. With no one to keep the fires going, all our provisions would freeze. As usual in the fall we had ordered a winter's food supply, too much to let go to waste. Also, Ted had no time to secure the buildings. Wilderness cabins, particularly on the shore where they could be reached easily, were becoming vulnerable to looters and vandals.

The third reason was the boat, which I was beginning to hate. Ted had it up on a grid close to the embankment, with a ladder leading ashore. At high tide the water reached it and on the big tides once a month, it floated. It leaked and had to be pumped out at least every few days to keep it from filling and freezing. If that happened the fastenings would pull out and the planking would spring away from the ribs. My most important job and real reason for remaining at home was to save the boat.

Fortunately we now had a two-way short-wave radio set up in the house with 6-volt batteries and a battery charger that I could operate. We also had a supply of coal Ted had brought from the Homer side earlier in autumn, so fuel would be no problem. Ted had left the coal pile on the beach, as we had no easy way of hauling freight up to the cabin. I still wore the back brace and wasn't supposed to lift more than 25 pounds, but I didn't mind making several trips a day up the trail with small loads.

Roxy, across the ridge, was also alone that winter. She had a short-wave radio, too, and we talked to each other daily. They had converted their potato field to a landing strip, and we cooperated on the expense of having our mail flown in from Homer twice a month. With that shift in mailing address we lost the library service provided by Susan English in Seldovia. To substitute, I often sent orders for paperback books to the Book Cache in Anchorage, leaving the selection to the good judgment of Doris Riemann, who never failed her bush customers all over Alaska.

I had another radio friend with whom I talked every morning. Flora and Joel Moss, who lived at Peterson Bay down Kachemak from Halibut Cove, were friends of long standing, and Flora and I called each other daily. Joel fished for the company I worked for and kept a boat in the water all winter, and in case of emergency I knew he would come to my assistance.

I was thankful that we had a regular mail schedule, remembering how haphazardly we had gotten our mail in the early years of homesteading. I usually hiked over the hill with the outgoing mail the day before the plane was expected, and Ted went a day later for the incoming mail. Most of our clothing and household goods were supplied by mail order houses. A package from Sears, Roebuck, or L.L. Bean was like a gift even though we had ordered and paid for it. That winter when I was alone, mail days were more than ever highlights, as they gave me an excuse to visit with Roxy. Even though we had a lot of snow that year and I had to trudge through the woods on snowshoes, I always looked forward to it.

With no work to do outdoors except to carry in coal and water and shovel snow out of the paths to the creek, beach and outhouse—and keep the boat pumped out—I had plenty of time to read and write. The Cove was completely iced over so no one could come along the beach. Occasionally I walked over to the Newman place just to look across open water and to break a snowshoe trail in case anyone wanted to walk in to see me. I had spells of loneliness but consoled myself that we were not going deeper into debt.

That winter of 1957 I finished the book. It was an expansion of a serial titled "Alaska Boy" that I had written for the Methodist Sunday School publication *Boys Today*. With a hopeful heart I sent it to a publisher, then settled back to wait.

Changes were taking place in the North Pacific fishery, starting late in the 1950s. Although he did not live to see it, Kinky Alexander's dream of a king crab industry in Alaska was beginning to be realized by others. In Seldovia the cold storage plant began to process king crabs for a few months at the end of the salmon season.

Charles "Chuck" Hendrix was the plant superintendent. From the time I started to work in Seldovia, he and his wife Candida were my good friends. For a time I shared a duplex with them, and the door between our quarters was never locked and seldom closed. Their little girls, Tracy and Kay, were my friends, and Tracy became my special pet. When I took the cannery wagon to the post office to pick up packages she often rode along, and she trudged by my side on other errands when they were not too far from the office.

I became the cold storage bookkeeper when my season closed the end of August 1957 in the salmon cannery office. A winter operation was out of the question, as the buildings were not intended for cold weather operations and by mid-October the water lines froze. The fishing fleet, small local boats that fished mainly in Kachemak Bay, were also not equipped to fish in winter weather.

Ted went back on the *Expansion* a second year, and this time I moved to Seward for the winter. While half a winter alone on the homestead had not been bad, I was not willing to go back and stay alone all winter. Ted nailed up the warehouse and the cabin and took the boat to Seward, where he hauled it up on the beach for the winter. Friends drove me to Seward from Homer when the king crab operation came to an end.

Alaska Boy had been rejected. I still had faith that it was publishable and planned to send it out again. During the summer the Methodist minister in Seldovia had mentioned to me that Abingdon Press was part of the Methodist Publishing House. Since my short stories and serials had been well-received by this publisher, I reasoned they might also accept the book. As soon as I got to Seward and rented a post office box so I had a return address, I sent the manuscript to Abingdon Press in Nashville, Tennessee.

Luckily for me, I had a good friend in Seward, Pat Williams, daughter of L.V. and Hazel Ray, family friends of Ted's. Since Pat's insurance office was in the same building as my apartment, we saw each other every day.

Pat recommended me to the Seward city manager, who was looking for a secretary. Within a few days Bill Bordwell hired me and I spent the winter working in City Hall. Mr. Bordwell's keen mind and sardonic sense of humor made my job a pleasure. The *Expansion* was in port only a few days every month, so I lived alone most of the time but had friends and co-workers for company.

Again, with both of us working our financial situation improved. We took another step to put our affairs in better order. With the salmon fishery dwindling, one of the fish plants in Seldovia ceased operation, while two others, Seldovia Bay Packing Company and Alaska Year Round Canneries, consolidated. The cannery building in which I had worked was converted entirely to the cold storage business, packing halibut and king crab. Ted had no particular attachment to the consolidation, and in order not to be tied to them by our debt, we applied for a Small Business Administration loan to refinance our boat obligation. We got our loan and were committed to pay a fixed amount every year. To me, this was better than repaying a percentage of the money Ted might earn with the boat.

The work at Seward City Hall was pleasant and interesting. Pat and I visited often and our friendship became close and permanent. I made few other real friends and had very little social life, but spent my free time writing. During this period I started a series of articles on communities on the Kenai Peninsula, which were published in *The Alaska Sportsman* magazine.

For the Soldotna article I went to Sterling and Walt drove me around to talk to people. He also took photographs, and the article was published under both our names. This had an odd result. The article was read by one of Walt's half-sisters, Lydia Hunter. She had lost track of Walt when he was eight years old. Through Lydia, Walt was drawn back into his family circle, relatives through his mother who had had no connection with Ted.

One day that winter I went to pick up my mail and before opening the post office box saw that dreaded thick brown envelope through the little window in the door to the box. My manuscript had been returned again. Disheartened and depressed, I went home for lunch, threw the unopened package on the sofa, and glowered at it occasionally as I ate.

What was wrong with me? Was I wasting my time, thinking I could write? I should forget it and try something else. A lot of time and effort had been invested in that manuscript, all apparently wasted. I decided to file the package on the shelf with my other writing material, and come to some decision about whether or not to go on writing.

As I glared at the offending manila envelope it gradually occurred to me that something was strange. For a moment I puzzled, then the answer hit me. That package had been returned to me by airmail! I certainly hadn't put airmail stamps on the self-addressed envelope I had sent with the manuscript. This was very peculiar.

Hastily I tore open the package. A letter from the editor was inside. She liked my book! She wanted to publish it! She had noted on the manuscript the changes she wanted me to make. Would I rewrite and return the revised manuscript?

Would I! After initial dismay at all the cuts, I set to work following her suggestions. I trusted her to know her business and later could see she improved my work. Sometimes

I wondered, with a little shiver, what would have happened to my writing career if I hadn't opened that package before filing it.

About this time I made my first contact with other Alaska writers. In the newspaper I read that the League of Alaska Writers was holding a conference and the public was invited. At that meeting I met Chris McClain, Margaret Mielke, Phyllis Carlson, Frances Anater and others who, like me, were struggling for literary recognition. The program was interesting, with talks by author and playwright Frank Brink and commercial photographer Ward Wells, and poetry readings by members of the League.

I did not then and do not to this day believe in discussing my work in progress. Writing is an extremely personal affair and as far as I'm concerned is not a debatable subject. I think of Sinclair Lewis, when asked to address a group of aspiring writers. He stalked across the stage and stood glaring over the podium.

"So you want to be writers?" he demanded. "Then why aren't you home writing?" That was the end of his speech.

Workshops, where manuscripts are read and criticized by others, are not for me. To me, this is the blind leading the blind. When group participants are on the same level of accomplishment, they are not qualified to judge each others' work. A subtle atmosphere of "You praise my work, I'll praise yours" may creep in. Jealousy and malice can also enter the scene, and a potential writer might be crushed by spiteful criticism.

The writers league soon disbanded, but I kept in touch with Chris McClain and Phyllis Carlson. In later years the Alaska Press Women organized, and although my visits to Anchorage were few and far between, whenever I was in town some of these friends gathered for lunch with me. My circle of writing acquaintances broadened to include Lenore

Hedla, Betzi Woodman, Wendy Jones, Sylvia Munsey and others.

Writing books opened an entirely new world for me. My first book, re-titled *Victory at Bear Cove,* was published in the autumn of 1958. It was a beautiful book, illustrated by a well-known artist, Edward Shenton. My only disappointment was that my name was misspelled on the dust jacket, although not on the book itself. I was thrilled with the attention given me, while trying to retain my sense of proportion.

Everyone seemed to rejoice with me. Susan English, as Seldovia librarian, sponsored a reception and most of my friends attended. In Anchorage, Beatrice Culver, whose husband still owned the fox farm at Bear Cove, helped organize an autograph party at the old Book Cache, which shared a log building with a natural history museum on Sixth Avenue. I was pleased to be asked for my autograph, and am to this day.

Ted was happy for me, too, and bragged about me to his friends and acquaintances. Whenever anyone complimented me in his presence, however, he usually threw a dash of cold water by admonishing me later, "Now don't let it go to your head."

My father's reaction was typical of him. All my life, from the time I brought home A's on my report card, I had hoped to hear him say, "Elsa, I'm proud of you." When I sent him a copy of my book I was sure the time had come. Instead he wrote me, "It's a nice little book, and maybe some day you'll write something you can really be proud of."

My contract with Abingdon Press stipulated that my next two books be submitted to them first, although they were not committed to accept them. I took that to mean I was to send them another manuscript as soon as possible, and I started a new book immediately.

While my friends were thrilled and happy for my success, the reaction of a crew member on the mailboat *Expansion* wasn't so kind. Ted proudly presented the captain an autographed copy in the presence of some of the crew.

"Uh-oh," one of them said derisively. "You know what this means. Your wife's going to kick up her heels the way that woman in the East is doing. Elsa's going to look for a younger husband too."

He was referring to the escapades of Grace Metalious, after the enormous success of her novel *Peyton Place*. She had divorced her husband and married a much younger man, and her private affairs were spread across the pages of newspapers and magazines nationwide. Ted didn't seem to take the teasing to heart, but it dimmed my pleasure a little.

Herring Pete
and His Jo

TED WAS happy finally to be out on his own boat, but his first solo salmon fishing venture was unsuccessful. From his cannery tender experience he knew how to locate the fish, but he had no experience catching them. I suggested he take along an experienced fisherman to teach him, but he did not agree. The main reason he had gotten the boat was to work alone, in his own way. Besides, he had watched other fishermen make big fishing paydays and saw no reason he could not do the same.

He didn't even make expenses. Since we had that boat loan to pay, he went back on the Aleutian mail run another winter, and I went along with him to Seward in his boat.

That voyage, and the return in the spring, were the best

trips I ever made in his boat. The weather was glorious and the scenery around the southern perimeter of the Kenai Peninsula was spectacular.

Towering cliffs reared out of the sea, separated by expanses of primeval forest. Torrents of water fell over the rocks like bridal lace, while conical peaks thrust out of the distant Harding ice field, with icy tongues licking down the gaps in the mountain range. We saw tiny white specks in grassy pockets in the cliffs that turned into mountain goats when we studied them through binoculars.

The sea itself teemed with life. Seabirds by the thousands screamed and dived over schools of fish. Gulls flew by to study us arrogantly, as though about to demand a bucket of garbage. A school of porpoises appeared and leaped exuberantly on either side of our bow. The final excitement was a couple of whales that breached and crashed back into the sea ahead of us.

We stayed overnight at the fox farm of Pete and Josephine Sather on Nuka Island. We both knew Herring Pete through dealing with him in the fisheries, but Jo was a new acquaintance to me, although Ted knew her from cannery tender days. In my mind she has become the epitome of a lonely wilderness woman.

Jo Sather had come to Nuka Island with her first husband many years before I met her, to raise blue foxes. The breeding stock they brought ran wild on the island, foraging on the beaches and on the salmon, seals and other carcasses brought to them. They grew quite wild, but we caught glimpses of their descendants and heard them bark during the calm moonlit night. Jo and Pete no longer set box traps to catch the foxes they once slaughtered for the pelts. Pete still beachcombed feed for the foxes, but in recent years they had become pets and no longer a source of income.

Jo and her first husband had built a house that gradually

grew into a dwelling that would not have been out of place in Jo's native Austria. In a lot of ways Jo Sather reminded me of Roxy Pomeroy, not only for her European accent but also because she could do everything, from carpentry to gardening, raising chickens to skinning foxes and caring for the pelts. Her energy seemed inexhaustible, although she complained that advancing age was slowing her down.

Her house was cluttered with the accumulation of years of mail order shopping. China cabinets were loaded with fancy dishes, ornaments and photos of exotic places, some sent by people who had enjoyed her hospitality, some she had ordered herself. Oil paintings decorated the walls; she had carpets on the floors and plush upholstered furniture. She made big rag rugs and crocheted doilies to cover the tables and chair arms and backs.

The first years at Nuka Island had not been too lonely for her. The gold mines on the mainland at Nuka Arm and East Arm were in operation, with mail and supply boats stopping frequently at the fox farm. While she rarely saw a woman, for the miners' wives stayed in town, boat crews were always welcomed with a meal or at least with a mug-up.

When her husband died, Jo tried to make it alone on the island. She couldn't manage to do so, and when Pete Sather, operator of one of the boats that carried freight for the mines, suggested they marry and join forces, she agreed.

They were a strange couple. Where Pete was a slight man with a round gargoyle face, Jo was thick and sturdy. Where she was assertive in manner he was quiet and shy except when he drank, which was whenever he made a trip to town. Jo was immaculate in dress and in her house, which she kept vividly painted and scrubbed to a shine. Herring Pete, on the other hand, could live happily on his boat for weeks with a limited supply of fresh water and no soap. Jo told me she made him bathe and change clothes before she let him in the house after one of his fishing trips. Remembering the aura of halibut slime and salmon gurry that surrounded him when he came into the fish plant office, I didn't blame her.

Although we had barely met, Jo poured out her life history to me. Thinking of my own first years on the homestead at Bear Cove, I could sympathize with her. More than anything she wanted to talk to another woman. I also recognized in her one of my own failings. From listening to men gossiping over coffee mugs when they stopped at the homestead, I would glean small bits of unrelated information about people and happenings. Then in my mind I would weave theories of probable reasons and occurrences, which later almost always proved to be in error. So it was with Jo Sather. She told me things she had heard about people I knew in Seldovia and Seward that I knew to be completely erroneous.

She emphasized to me that her relationship with Herring Pete was one of business, with no romance involved. She provided him with a good home, while he hunted for fox feed, whether by shooting seals, salvaging a sea lion or killer whale carcass washed up on some beach, or gathering spawned-out, rotting salmon from the fish creeks on the mainland. He did all the errands in town and carried the mail, while she did the housework and most of the maintenance around the Nuka Island place. They had separate bank accounts and kept scrupulous track of their expenses.

Despite her protestations, it was obvious there was a certain affection between them. She worried about him when he was away, on fishing trips for halibut and salmon, or when he went shopping or for mail to Seward and Seldovia. She knit heavy turtle-necked sweaters for him, and bullied him into ordering warm clothing and footgear. Knowing he rarely cooked on the boat except for poisonously strong cups of coffee, she made enormous, heavy doughnuts for him, crammed with whole wheat flour, raisins, sunflower seeds and everything else she thought would increase their nutrition.

Pete was very proud of Jo, and I heard some of his stories about her long before I met her. She was extremely possessive of her home and surrounding island, and fought off any encroachment. She had her own commercial fishing license, a seine and a skiff, and regarded any salmon that came into Home Cove as her personal property.

One summer evening before the fishing period for the week was to open at six the next morning, a school of pink salmon came into Home Cove and lay in the calm water off Jo and Pete's boat dock. Jo kept her eyes on them and prepared to make a set as soon as it was legal. Pete was away on his own fishing expedition and she was home alone.

Late in the evening the seine skiff of a notorious creek robber from Seldovia nosed into the cove and he saw the school of fish. Jo shouted to him, claiming the fish for herself, but the lawless fisherman lingered. She knew that as soon as she went to the house he would make the set and she would lose the fish.

Hastily she rushed to get her shotgun. She sat on the dock all night, the loaded gun across her lap. When it was legal to do so, she set her seine and held the fish surrounded until Pete came home to help her land them. To Pete it was a knee-slapping story, and he was fond of repeating it.

Pete was a kindly man. One time Ted heard him discussing the war and the dropping of the atom bomb on Japan. Kinky Alexander exclaimed, "Good! They should have killed all the Japs."

"No, no, Kinky," Pete protested in distress. "They are people, too."

Jo Sather had written her life story, and over my protests she insisted I take the manuscript to Seward to read and edit it. I did not consider myself a critic and could not be objective about another writer's work—and when I read her story I knew it would take more time than I wanted to give to prepare and submit it to a publisher. I had my own writing plans, with my second book already under way. I returned Jo Sather's manuscript to her the following spring on our way back to Seldovia.

When I sent my second book to the publisher at the end of winter, the editor liked it but was dismayed I had submitted another manuscript so soon. The publisher's policy was to issue an author's work only every two years. By the time I got that word, my third book was already started. Abingdon Press did accept the second book right away and published it a year after *Victory at Bear Cove.*

My contract with Abingdon Press stipulated I was to receive 8 percent of the selling price of each copy as my royalty payment. From reading professional publications I knew this was a modest, almost niggardly rate, and I felt I deserved better. In no position to bargain for myself, I needed an agent.

In *The Writer* magazine I found the name and address of an organization of literary agents the magazine considered reputable. I sent for their list of members and wrote to three of them chosen at random. One never answered. Another did not handle work for juvenile readers. The third, McIntosh and Otis of New York, replied that they would be pleased to handle my work, especially since I had already marketed one book manuscript myself. Their associate, Caroline Sauer, renegotiated my contract with Abingdon Press, and all my subsequent juvenile book manuscripts were placed with publishers by this firm of agents.

My second book was *Dangerous Flight,* an expansion of a six-part serial entitled "Alaska Adventure" and published in the *Young Catholic Messenger.* Abingdon Press editors did not like the original title and renamed the book. This caused some confusion among my friends, who asked about my "airplane book." Actually, the book was about two Yankee seafarers shipwrecked on the Alaska coast and their struggle to escape the persecution of a Russian fur trader, before the purchase of Alaska by the United States.

CHANGES CONTINUED in the fishing business in the early 1960s. Salmon was no longer the primary resource. In Seldovia only one salmon cannery remained, and that one consolidated with the cannery at Port Graham for a season. For one summer the only substantial Seldovia fisheries plant was the cold storage plant, which processed halibut during the spring and summer and king crabs in the fall. In addition, a shrimp cannery struggled to get into production on a very limited basis. Then the Port Graham cannery burned to the beach and the consolidated salmon canning operation moved back to Seldovia.

King crab fishing was of prime importance in the little community. The old Squeakey Anderson cold storage plant had been sold to Wakefield Fisheries, pioneers in the crab fishery. The Alaska Shellfish plant, originally built by Kinky Alexander, was now canning king crab. The Alaska Year Round cannery packed only salmon for the Seldovia-Port Graham Consolidation, and the shrimp processing firm had taken over the reduction plant building and was canning shrimp.

Along with Chuck Hendrix and other administrative employees, I stayed with Wakefield Fisheries in the old cold storage plant and salmon cannery, stripped of its packing lines. The crab packing operation extended into October, so I was working in Seldovia seven months a year and sometimes longer.

Ted, thoroughly sick of the Aleutian mail run, quit his job. By nature he was not suited to the close confinement of shipboard life for long periods of time. For a few years he went salmon fishing in the summer and crab fishing in the fall, and we spent the winter months on the homestead.

At this time, writing became the most important interest in my life. *Victory at Bear Cove* eventually sold over 10,000 copies. *Dangerous Flight* didn't do as well. Book number three, *Alaska Harvest,* was in some ways my most successful book.

Like other books I wrote, it evolved through several stages. It started as a serial published by *Girls Today,* the Methodist Sunday School magazine. Three years later it was published by Lantern Press in their anthology *Teen Age Small Boat Stories*. Still later, the serial was printed in the textbook *The New Open Highways,* describing various occupations from astronaut to commercial fisherman.

Expanded to book length, *Alaska Harvest* went through several editions printed by Abingdon Press, sales totaling 12,000 copies. The book also had two editions by Cadmus Press, a firm specializing in hardbound books for school use. With three books in print and earning royalties, I felt I could finally call myself a writer.

My last book for Abingdon Press was *Mountain of the Sun,* another story set in the days of the Russian era in Alaska. This book was popular with Alaskans but did not do well in the other states. Total sales amounted to only 4,200 copies.

At about the time *Mountain of the Sun* came out, Ted and I faced another change. His fishing ventures were not the success he had hoped, and it took all our efforts to meet the boat debt payments. When we heard that a watchman was needed at a shut-down herring processing plant in the Kodiak area, Ted applied and was hired. The salary was modest, almost a pittance, but included board and room for both of us so at least we would not be going into debt over the winter.

Ted thought this would be a good chance to work on the boat, doing the inside cabin work and other improvements that had not been finished. We took along all the tools and the materials he would need, expecting to have plenty of time during the winter to do the boat work. We set off from Seldovia in a cheerful frame of mind, headed for another adventure.

By the time we reached the mouth of Cook Inlet the worst storm of the year was generating in the North Pacific. A wide expanse of open water between the Kenai Peninsula and the Kodiak islands lay before us, and Ted decided not to risk being caught in a storm.

We took shelter in Port Chatham on the southwest tip of the Kenai Peninsula, along with several other boats. As we lay there at anchor for several days waiting for the storm to pass, we heard on the boat radio band about the search that was under way for Herring Pete Sather. He had left Seward for Nuka Bay before we left Seldovia, and Coast Guard inquiries had already started before I left the fish plant office. All boats in the area were alerted to look for him, and search parties went out from Seward.

He was never found. After waiting in vain for months, his wife Jo sold her place on the island and went to Seattle. Later she went back to her Austrian homeland, where she died. Herring Pete was only the first of a dozen Alaska fishermen who lost their lives that stormy winter.

PORT VITA, on Raspberry Island in the Kodiak group, was a spooky place. Abandoned for many years, the buildings stood open to the weather and were decaying. The main plant was three stories high, with great cavernous rooms, shadowy and filled with antiquated machinery.

The purpose of the plant had been to pack the largest and best of the herring catch into barrels with salt, to press the oil out of the smaller fish and the gurry through a cooking process, and to dry the residue into fish meal. Once the herring fishery ended, there was no further use for the plant. The owners kept a watchman there only to satisfy the requirements of the insurance company. The place was like a little town, all moss-grown and mouldering. Separate bunkhouses for men and women had been built on the slope above the main plant, along with cottages for managers and foremen. There were a commissary, mess hall and offices in another building, and a superintendent's house overlooked the entire site.

Port Vita was the center of three herring plants along Raspberry Strait. Each fish plant salted herring and cooked out fish oil, which was piped to Port Vita through heavy rubber hoses that lay on the ground between the three plants, to be refined before shipment to Seattle. The plant at Iron Creek, off Shelikof Strait, finally burned down. On the opposite end of Raspberry Island was Port Wakefield; its herring plant had evolved into the king crab company that bought the plant in Seldovia. A trail and a primitive, overgrown road connected the three plants.

Port Vita seemed to be filled with ghosts, and I knew a little about them. Olaf Floe was nephew and bookkeeper to the man who had owned the herring plant at Iron Creek. He told me about those herring days that were the heyday of Alaska fishing before the boom years of the king crab fishery.

Large seine boats, each crewed by half a dozen men, came up from Puget Sound and British Columbia to fish in the North Pacific. The size of the herring runs was almost unimaginable, with packing plants not only on Raspberry Strait but in other locations on the Kodiak islands and several in Seldovia and Kachemak Bay. Old ships, condemned from carrying freight and lumber, were towed up and anchored near the fishing grounds and used as floating salteries.

Halibut Cove was the site of a number of these saltery plants, as well as the Tutka Bay plant that Ted had torn down. It was said that when the fleet anchored for the night in Kachemak Bay, mast lights and running lights on the seiners gave the bay the look of a small city.

Processing the catch of all those boats required more plant workers than Alaska villages could supply. Men and women were brought up from Seattle and elsewhere to work in the plants. The women gutted the herring and prepared them for salting while the men did the heavier work—unloading the boats, operating the reduction machinery, maintaining the buildings, making and repairing the fishing gear and setting up the enormous wood-staved tierces to hold the salted fish.

Many of the plant workers and fishermen were young, and impromptu parties bubbled up frequently. In addition, a dance was held every Saturday night at Port Vita, the central location between the three plants. Musicians among the workers and fishermen formed a small band and provided the dance music, and the large, smooth and slippery floor of the web loft on the third story of the plant provided the place. Standing in the shadowy room, I could sense the hilarity that must have rung among the rafters during those herring days.

There was no warning when the herring fishery came to an end. One year the fishermen caught their usual tons of herring, and the plants all along the North Pacific Rim processed the usual amount of salted fish, oil and fish meal. The workers and fishermen came back the following spring, ready for another bounteous season, but the herring didn't show up.

The herring industry crashed. Plants were abandoned or

converted to other uses. Herring seiners became halibut boats or cannery tenders. Not for many years were there herring runs in more than meager amounts. Like the disappearance of vast king crab schools in later years, the reason remained a mystery.

TWELVE

Another 80 Acres

OUR WINTER in Port Vita was a productive one for me, but less so for Ted. He had brought all his power tools to work on the boat, but found there was no electricity to power them. The generator in the watchman's house was barely large enough to furnish electricity for domestic lights and water pump. The herring plant machine shop was still fully equipped with everything he might need for his boat-building work, but the enormous diesel power plant stood lifeless and rusting.

What was worse, we discovered that the Port Vita dock was no place to tie up the boat for the winter. Strong winds gusted up and down Raspberry Strait and churned the water to a froth. Ted put out a mooring in Selief Bay beyond Port

Wakefield where he tied up the boat. All winter he rowed back and forth the two miles, carefully choosing a lull in the weather, to keep the boat pumped out.

The stormy weather that kept us indoors was a break for me. I was writing a book about salmon driftnet fishing in Cook Inlet, and Ted was handy to advise me on technical details. This book became *Cook Inlet Decision* and I dedicated it to Ted, acknowledging his assistance.

This book was to me my most beautiful book and I am especially proud of it. The woodcut illustrations and jacket design by Walter Ferro were outstanding and caught the spirit of the book particularly well. It eventually went into several Atheneum Publishers and Cadmus Press editions and was on the *New York Times* list of 100 best books for young people in 1963.

Years later an amateur movie maker came to me, requesting the use of *Cook Inlet Decision* as the plot for a film he wanted to make about salmon fishing. Since the copyright was owned by Atheneum Publishers I referred him to them, indicating I was willing to go along with his venture. The publisher did not share my confidence and refused his request, so the film was never made.

Because we had worked together while I wrote my book, I had hopes that at last Ted would start his book, *White Wilderness*. He went so far as to clean up a cabin adjoining the house where we lived at Port Vita to use as a study. I offered my assistance as typist, then suggested we collaborate on some other story to give him the feel for writing. He declined to work with me and I decided never to mention his book again.

There was not much to do at Port Vita after we had explored the buildings and the trails that still connected the three plants. Our mail came to Port Wakefield, the headquarters and main processing plant for Wakefield Fisheries, and we got our groceries at their commissary. We walked over every few days, and sometimes visited with friends that I had made through working in the company's Seldovia plant.

During the winter I had an interesting trip provided by Wakefield Fisheries. The bookkeeper at the company's Sand Point plant was having problems balancing her books. Since I knew the system, the company auditor asked me to go out for a few days to give her a hand.

The company field man and I flew to Kodiak on the local mail plane to catch the Reeve Aleutian plane that would continue to the Westward. This plane was loaded with passengers headed for the Navy base at Adak, and we were lucky to get seats. Before we could claim them we were weighed, along with our luggage, to make sure we would not overload the plane, which had nearly reached its maximum capacity.

Sand Point, in the Shumagin Islands near the end of the Alaska mainland, has a climate like that of the Aleutians. The only trees, a little grove of stunted spruce trees, had been planted in a sheltered spot by some early settler. Alders were the island's main shrubbery, and they grew long and close to the ground, their serpentine limbs beat down by the ceaseless wind.

The Shumagin Islands are windier than Raspberry Strait. When we went from the superintendent's house to the crab plant on the dock, we joined hands and walked close together to keep from being blown off the boardwalk. I left there during a lull in the weather and flew back to Port Vita by way of Anchorage.

With so much writing time that winter, I finished the salmon fishing book well before spring and had time on my hands. I wrote several articles on the North Pacific fisheries for boating magazines but wanted to do a longer work. The setting of Port Vita, with its scabrous and decaying buildings, the over-grown, moss-hung forest, the constantly threatening weather, prompted me to write a mystery book.

Mystery on Malina Strait was the result, *malina* being the Russian word for salmonberries that grew lushly on the island and were mistaken for raspberries by later settlers. This was a book for younger children and was accepted through my agent by Ives Washburn, Publishers.

The strong winds that so depressed me increased to hurricane force one early spring day. We shivered in our uninsulated, poorly heated house. When finally the storm blew itself out and Ted made a round of inspection, he found that one side of the main building had caved in during the storm. When he telephoned the news to the Seattle office he was told to clean up the wreckage and enclose the building as best he could. He agreed to accept whatever material he could salvage as payment for this extra work.

Ted was in his glory. This plant, like the one at Tutka Bay closer to home, had been built when clear, straight-grained and knot-free lumber was readily available. Even with nail holes and notches it was better than most lumber on the market now. He was given permission to hire a small crew of men from a nearby village. Ted put aside all the long 2 x 8 planks they saved to take back to Bear Cove.

At Iron Creek, where the plant had been destroyed by fire many years before, he had found an enormous, wide, flat-bottomed herring seine skiff hauled up in the weeds and abandoned. He salvaged, repaired and painted it and launched it with great effort, to carry his salvaged lumber back to Bear Cove.

On our voyage home we were heavily laden with Ted's booty, in both the boat hold and the herring skiff, which trailed behind us on a towline. The skiff gave us trouble from the start. We had to stop and drift several times, so Ted could adjust the load to get the right trim and keep the skiff towing properly, not yawing from side to side. We had timed our departure from Port Vita so we would have the benefit of a flooding tide through Shelikof Strait and on into Cook Inlet. The towing troubles delayed us.

By the time darkness closed around us we were not yet through the strait. We had run out of the fair tide and our progress slowed to a crawl as the tide turned against us. Ted thought about anchoring in Shuyak Strait, the last shelter in the Kodiak islands, but decided against it. With the weather still calm he decided any progress we made was to our advantage, and by the time we reached the Barren Islands, halfway to Seldovia, the tide would be flooding again.

Halfway to the Barrens the wind picked up. The sky was overcast so we lost the benefit of even the faint starlight. We knew a scattering of rock pinnacles peppered the sea south of the Barren Islands. We kept watch from the pilothouse windows with strained intensity, as the boat wallowed in the tide rips. Something in the cabin caught my attention. I glanced behind me, down the scuttle.

"Fire!" I screamed. "The boat's on fire!"

"Take the wheel!" Ted ordered.

I clutched the gyrating spokes while he grabbed a fire extinguisher and disappeared down into the cabin.

Fighting the wheel as the waves threw the boat around, I frantically looked for rocks ahead. Expecting the engine to die at any moment, I thought of the scores of tragedies at sea I had heard about during my years in the fishery. So this is how it is going to end, I thought, remembering Herring Pete and all the other fishermen who had perished at sea in the past year.

My despair was premature. The starter solenoid had malfunctioned and become so overheated that the paint and film of oil on the engine caught fire. Ted put it out with the fire extinguisher and the engine kept running. We finally saw the Barren Islands looming ahead and anchored in the only shelter available. We lay there the rest of the night and most of the next day. The wind continued. We didn't talk much. I tried not to think what would have happened if we had hit one of those half-submerged rocks or had been unable to put out the fire.

We were in touch with Seldovia by radio and learned that the Barren wind was only local and weather conditions in lower Cook Inlet were generally fine. In the afternoon on the flooding tide we set out on the next leg of our voyage. It was nearly midnight when we finally tied up at the Seldovia Boat Float. Ted headed for the tavern while I went to the Hendrix home where Chuck and Candy awaited us. I cried when I told them what had happened, choking back hysteria. They tried to soothe me with assurances that the fire had been a freak mishap, but I had permanently lost confidence and never had another boat trip with Ted that I really enjoyed.

THE SUMMER after we returned from Port Vita I was offered the job of Seldovia town clerk. It was a half-day job and I filled out the working day in the office of the cold storage plant. Since Chuck Hendrix was the mayor as well as the plant superintendent, in a sense I worked for him full-time.

Seldovia was beset by problems brought on by year-round plant operations. The water distribution system was inadequate and there was no public sewer system. A rock jetty had been built enclosing the mouth of the slough that emptied into the harbor in front of the town. The boat harbor was of great benefit to the fishermen, who now kept their boats in the water the year around to fish for crabs, instead of hauling them out for the winter at the end of the salmon season. The rock jetty, however, impeded the flow of the tides that had formerly kept the beaches flushed off.

All the houses along the slough and the waterfront, and many on the surrounding slopes as well, had sewer pipes running down to the beach and emptying into the harbor. The small boat harbor became an open sewer, flushed out only on the very highest tides once a month.

Garbage was another problem. Despite an ordinance forbidding the practice, many people simply threw their garbage over the boardwalk railing or off the cannery docks. At the plants, the gurry scows sometimes overflowed before they were towed out of the harbor and dumped. The beaches along the waterfront were littered all year long with shellfish waste as well as tin cans, plastic containers and broken liquor bottles. No longer could the residents be assured that the beaches would clean themselves in the winter. A windrow of crab and shrimp shells accumulated at the top of the beach, undisturbed by even the highest tides. On warm summer days the odor was powerful. Although the financial improvement to the residents brought on by an all-year fishery was welcome, it was offset by the many disadvantages created by prosperity.

At this time Ted and I had a serious situation in regard to our homestead claim. Like many others who had settled in a heavily wooded area, we found it almost impossible to clear and cultivate the required 10 acres of our 80 without heavy equipment. To make matters worse, now we were home only five winter months, when living conditions were especially difficult.

We had burned out as many stumps as we could while clearing land, but more of them remained. Birch, alder and spruce trees grew back as fast as we cleared new areas, especially in the bare spots where we had burned stumps.

When we still hadn't qualified for a title after our claim extension expired, we were afraid someone would come along and file over our claim, on the land we had cleared. In order to protect our rights to the cabin and surrounding area we applied for a five-acre homesite. Having already qualified, by the length of our residence and the improvements we made, we had no trouble getting our patent. I was satisfied with the amount of land we got. It meant security to me, and in truth we had no use for all the land we had originally claimed, since we found no way to make a living at Bear Cove.

Ted was unhappy when he saw the meager acreage encompassed within the survey lines. He wanted to make sure we got the "house hill," that knoll to the south of the cabin where he still planned to build a modern house some day. If we started the survey on that beach corner, however, the opposite line came down the slope between our cabin and the original foundation he had put in. This left several acres of land we had cleared and could no longer claim as ours. Also eliminated from our property was the ever-flowing spring where we got our drinking water.

Ted's solution was to file for another 80-acre homestead, surrounding the homesite that had already been deeded to us. This meant clearing more land and, more importantly, building a habitable house and living on the land at least seven months for each of three years.

This seemed to me one way to get the modern house Ted had planned ever since we settled at Bear Cove. With all the lumber salvaged from Tutka Bay and Port Vita, surely we had enough material to build a house.

It was true Ted had enough dimensional lumber for the sills, joists, rafters and wall framing. He had also accumulated a vast amount of shiplap and siding from Tutka Bay, but it had been bundled and left lying on the edge of the woods, so it rotted in spots and he wouldn't use it.

We had to get a building up, in order to validate our new homestead claim. I had received a small inheritance from my father's estate, enough to buy plywood and paneling for the walls, windows, roofing and floor covering, as well as hardware and kegs of nails. One of our fisherman friends brought the building materials up from Seattle on his large crab boat, so the freight cost us nothing. To save time, Ted decided to use the foundation of our first log cabin that had never been finished and was over the border of our homesite.

I was happy to see the walls go up, with great progress visible every day. Since the foundation was only 12 x 18 feet, Ted decided to build half of the house on that and later excavate in the rear, extend the foundation and double the size of the original structure. The house had a shed roof sloping toward the beach, with the top of the rear wall planned for the ridgepole when the back addition was built.

By winter he had the building enclosed and had started on the interior. He located and brought home a large pot-bellied heater so he had a warm place to work. He was building intricate cabinets and shelves in the corner of the kitchen when spring came on.

As the snow started to melt and water ran down the slope, Ted was dismayed at the soggy area behind the new house. He decided that the location was unsuitable. The new house would have to be moved or dismantled and erected elsewhere. He stopped working on the new house while trying to decide what to do.

THIRTEEN

Year-Round Town Life

ONE EARLY spring day when the earth was still covered with snow, a jet fighter plane circled the Cove repeatedly. Since these planes usually flew in pairs on the occasions when we saw them swoop over on patrol or maneuvers, we feared that one pilot had crashed in the area and his partner was marking the spot until help arrived. We watched, listened and waited, but when nothing happened we went on with our work.

In the afternoon Harold Pomeroy came trudging over the ridge to tell us that the Culver house had burned to the ground that morning. The plane had circled while reporting the fire to the Federal Aviation Authority in Homer, but nothing could be done to save the house.

The watchman's wife and children had escaped, dressed only in bathrobes and slippers. While her husband fought the blaze, the woman conceived the idea that the surrounding woods might burn and start a forest fire. She had rushed over the hill to warn the Pomeroys. Since she was about my size, while Roxy was much smaller, Pom had come to borrow some clothes for her. They had saved nothing from the house except the two-way radio which the watchman had ripped from the wall.

The remodeling of Lillian Leonardt's house had never been completed. When Ben Culver and the carpenter split their partnership, the construction job was less than half done. The new stairway that led to the second floor had not yet been enclosed, and the wide opening cut into one outside wall to join the new part to the old house still gaped open, covered only by a canvas.

When the second story was added to the original building, a new hole had been cut through the ceiling between the two stories and through the roof to accommodate the chimney of the front room heater. The carpenter had left before he finished the stove assembly and had not had time to insulate the stovepipe between the floors or under the roof.

A late-winter cold spell had hit Bear Cove, and at the old fox farm the watchman struggled to heat the house. With the many openings in wall and ceiling, this was almost impossible. He was an impetuous man, and seeing his wife and children shivering, he lost his temper and continued to throw more wood into the heater.

Soon the chimney glowed with heat so intense the wood surrounding the pipe between floors caught fire. A few minutes later the house was in flames.

The exclusive lodge Ben Culver envisioned had gone up in smoke as insubstantial as all his dreams. Within a few months he was dead. His wife struggled to keep the place. Later we learned that after many years of receiving no payments, the father of the Fairbanks woman who originally bought the place from Leonardts had lost his patience and repossessed the property, since he had originally financed the purchase. It has since been subdivided into recreational lots, but only a few new places have been built.

That summer Ted went fishing for the last time, while I worked in the salmon cannery office and then went back to the cold storage plant in September. Our financial situation was perilous. Once more we didn't have enough for a winter grubstake and a boat payment.

Captain Thomsen still had the mail contract to the Aleutian Islands but had gone into the king crab processing business at Dutch Harbor, using the mail boat *Expansion* as a floating processing plant. He offered both of us a job, but Ted, seriously at odds with Thomsen's right-hand man, refused to join the enterprise. He did accept Thomsen's offer to run a smaller boat to carry the mail until the contract expired in a few months.

Since the Wakefield Fisheries plant in Seldovia now operated the year around, I became a permanent instead of a seasonal employee. I rented a small house in town and settled down. Ted hauled his boat up on a beach in Seldovia and secured it.

The mailboat job lasted a couple of trips. Ted was back in Seldovia when the Standard Oil Company tanker *Alaska Standard* came into port. Ted looked up the mate and applied for a job. He was given no great encouragement, the mate explaining that they rarely had vacancies on the ship and most of the hiring was done out of the Seattle office. It was all the more surprising, therefore, when a few days later I got a radio call from the *Alaska Standard*.

Two crewmen had quit unexpectedly. There was a job for Ted if he could get to Seward the next day. He jumped at the chance and was signed on as a deckhand.

Suddenly we were able to make double payments on our boat loan, and within a few years we were out of debt. Ted started buying things for the homestead while I bought government bonds to put away for our declining years.

I enjoyed becoming a permanent resident of Seldovia. Through my work in the processing plants I knew everyone. Chuck Hendrix was still mayor as well as superintendent of the main processing plant in town, and industry executives, government people and everyone else who came to town eventually called at our office.

The previous winter, my last on the homestead for more than five years, I had written *Fisherman's Choice*. This was the story of a homestead boy who had to choose between the meager life on his father's remote homestead and the exciting experiences of a crewman on a crab fishing boat. The book was accepted by Atheneum Publishers and went through several editions. Cadmus Press also published a school edition and most exciting of all, it was chosen as a Junior Literary Guild selection.

A few years later it came out in the United Kingdom, along with *Cook Inlet Decision,* which was retitled *Salmon Boat Sailor.* The books were edited slightly to conform with British language usage. The word "wrench" became "spanner," for instance, and "undershirt" became "vest," with additional changes of wording more familiar to British readers. The books were smaller in size and shape and the illustrations quite different from the United States editions.

During my summers in Seldovia I had sometimes sent news items to the *Anchorage Daily Times*. This was done as a favor to the Chamber of Commerce, to which I belonged. They wanted publicity for the little town, which was thriving as a result of the active crab and shrimp fishery. When I settled in Seldovia year-round I wrote a bylined column every week.

At this time Seldovia was splitting at the seams. Residents who once went Outside at the end of every fishing season now remained while fathers and sons participated in the winter fishery and many of the women worked in the processing plants. The more enterprising families bought larger boats, while newcomers to the fisheries were always available to take over the smaller craft that had originally been built and used only for salmon fishing.

Every livable house was occupied. Many had been built strictly for summer use and were hardly more than airy shacks. No matter—with four walls and a roof any house was rented or sold. These places, usually very small, had exposed water pipes and no insulation, so very cold weather meant difficulties. The house I rented was in this category, and having an absentee landlord I had to cope as best I could. Fortunately the plant machinists were friendly and would help solve my plumbing and heating problems when I couldn't.

That winter of 1963-64 was a peaceful one. With the Wakefield king crab freezer plant and the shrimp and king crab canneries operating, every woman and man who wanted work could find a job, in one of the plants or on one of the boats.

In my little house in the shadow of the Russian Church I was happy, too. The townspeople, always friendly and sociable, still maintained the old customs of entertaining themselves during the long winters with dinner parties, a pinochle tournament and much visiting back and forth. Birthdays were always a reason for celebration, with lavish gifts exchanged. The Christmas season stretched over nearly a month, from the middle of December through Russian Christmas and Russian New Year well into January. Through

my friendships with some of the old-timers and with cannery people, I was often included and for the first time felt I
was truly a resident of the town.

Until this time my image of myself was as an observer
rather than as a resident. Since formerly I had left town in
late fall when the fisheries plants closed, I was considered as
temporary as those who returned to Seattle at the end of the
season. Once I had rented a house, my status changed.

Socially I was in a peculiar position, always the single
person in a society of couples. I was careful not to be paired
with anyone, or to participate in the free-and-easy down-
town social life that was Seldovia's public image and revolved around the taverns. Seldovia had the reputation
among fishery people, executives as well as fishermen from
out of town, of being an uninhibited settlement, shielded
from the observation of the outside world, where conduct
not condoned elsewhere was uncensored and readily overlooked. While I was friendly with all who came to the office,
only people I knew well were invited to my home and I did
not encourage casual visitors.

During the first part of the winter I wrote another book
for younger children, *Mountain of Gold Mystery,* which was
published by Ives Washburn. When it came out I was col-
lecting royalties on seven books. The only other writing I
did was the weekly column for the Anchorage paper, with no
more magazine articles for many years. My schedule was to
get up early and write for two hours before going to the crab
plant office. I rarely went out on weekday evenings, as my
rising time was 5 a.m.

One Seldovia accomplishment that still gives me a sense
of pride was to co-found the Seldovia Hospital Guild. This
came about for two reasons.

For many years, before the construction of the Sterling
Highway, Seldovia had the only hospital on the western

Kenai Peninsula. It had been built in the early 1940s, and a doctor had been subsidized by various church missions and by the City of Seldovia. Women came from as far away as Kenai to have their babies or other hospital treatment, and the records show that in some years more than a hundred birth certificates were issued by the Seldovia magistrate.

When transportation to Anchorage improved and a hospital was built in Homer, Seldovia's facility served only the local people and a few from the outlying areas. It was extremely difficult to attract a competent doctor willing to serve so few people. The building was maintained by the city, but the equipment was somewhat obsolete. That was one spur to forming a hospital guild.

The second was my objection to the many fund-raising drives made in the town, mostly to benefit charities that never helped local people. One day, during a campaign for a medical society that I believed had only dubious credentials, I grumbled over a cup of coffee in Dorothy Parker's "The Galley" coffee shop.

"What we ought to do is raise money for some local cause," I remarked. "After all, charity begins at home."

Seldovia had a doctor at this time, who had been asking the city to invest in a good x-ray machine. Here was a cause that Seldovia women could adopt. I posted notices around town and about 20 women met in The Galley one evening, to organize the Seldovia Hospital Guild.

We were a little dismayed to learn that even a used x-ray machine would cost more than six thousand dollars. But a suitable machine was located by a hospital supplier recommended by the doctor, and the Guild went to work.

The entire town cooperated. Local businesses contributed; the seafood plants made substantial donations; the women had various fund-raising events. Olaf Floe, now purchasing agent for Wakefield Fisheries, sent us a sheaf of checks he had solicited from Seattle suppliers of fishing gear and equipment.

Within a fairly short time our x-ray machine was installed and paid for. Enthusiastic and proud of ourselves, we went on to buy and pay for a new typewriter for the hospital office and a new electric range for the doctor's living quarters in the basement of the hospital.

After 20 years, the Seldovia Hospital Guild is still active and a major organization in the town. In addition to assisting the health clinic with new equipment, the organization sponsors various social events, helps finance student scholarships and otherwise provides for the needs of people who cannot find help elsewhere.

FOURTEEN

Earthquake!

WHAT SEEMED an idyllic life in Seldovia was shattered on March 27, 1964. The Good Friday earthquake was so drastic that the little town near the mouth of Cook Inlet was never again the same. Most Alaskans who went through the experience are inclined to date events in their lives as "before the earthquake" and afterward. Not one person in the little town was unaffected.

Spring was already in the air that pre-Easter Friday. It was Chuck Hendrix's birthday, and a dinner party at his home was scheduled. I went up after work to set the table and otherwise give Candy a hand. She was busy in the kitchen while I sat by the dining table talking with her when the earthquake started. It began slowly and we were not alarmed. Earthquakes are fairly common on the Kenai Peninsula, and six months earlier we had had a jolt far stronger than the trembling now.

Within a few seconds, when the motion and rumbling did not cease, we knew that this quake was different. The hanging lamp over the dining table swayed violently and I grabbed it, while Candy dashed across the living room to keep a cupboard from toppling.

"This is a bad one," I gasped when the motion continued. While no official time was recorded of the earthquake's duration, unofficial timing ranged from three to four minutes, with some claims made that the original tremor continued for seven minutes. Stunned, we stared at each other in silence.

"The girls!" Candy exclaimed.

I headed for the door to search for them while Candy answered the telephone—it was Chuck calling from the plant office. Before I got through the doorway, Tracy and Kay ran into the yard, both screaming at full volume.

"Earthquake! Did you feel it? There are cracks across the back road!"

When we turned on the radio and all the Anchorage stations were off the air, we knew we were experiencing a disaster. Later we were to learn that the quake was the largest ever recorded on the North American continent. One hundred thirty-one people died, mostly from seismic sea waves.

The main shock was felt throughout Alaska and was centered in Prince William Sound. Seismic recording wells as far away as Georgia, Florida and Puerto Rico fluctuated markedly. People were washed away from a beach in Crescent City, California, by a seismic wave. Parts of the Kenai Mountains shifted sideways as much as five feet.

All this information did not reach us for a long time.

That Good Friday evening we knew only that we were cut off from the rest of Alaska, and that all of us were alive.

The guests invited to the birthday dinner gradually gathered, but no one felt like eating. Candy put the roast turkey and trimmings on the table and some of us nibbled distractedly, while others stuck with cocktails. The center of interest was the radio. One station in Anchorage with an auxiliary power plant soon came back on the air, but information was sparse. Most of the broadcast was warnings for the public to stay away from certain areas, and the pitiful appeals of people trying to locate family and friends.

The short-wave band was no more informative. The few boats on the air had as many questions as we did, most of them with no answers. On the high seas the boats were not affected by the tidal wave. One vessel kept calling anyone who might be listening, asking for information on Valdez. The plaintive questions went on and on late into the evening, with no one able to help since there had been no report from Prince William Sound, where damage was severe.

It was by boat short-wave radio later the next day that Wakefield Fisheries employees could assure relatives in the other states that we had survived. A list of next of kin was prepared and transmitted to one of the larger company fishing vessels on the North Pacific fishing grounds. The captain in turn relayed this information to the Wakefield Seattle office by way of the marine telephone operator, and our messages of reassurance were passed on.

The night of the quake every person in Seldovia was aware immediately that a greater danger threatened. A strong earthquake along the Alaska coast was often followed by a tidal wave, more accurately named a tsunami. I had already gone back to the office and gathered up the payroll, fishermen's records and checkbook and brought them to the

Hendrix house, which was on a knoll above the harbor. Other townspeople also gathered up their valuables. No one was surprised when, just after dark, the fire siren screamed its warning for people to go to higher ground.

I hastened to my little house, which was on a lower level nearer the waterfront, grabbed the metal box that contained Ted's and my valuable papers, and threw in the manuscript I was working on. In the other hand I clutched my portable radio, which had a short-wave band. Then I followed Candy and her girls to the schoolhouse high on the slope above the harbor, the traditional place of refuge for Seldovia people.

The classrooms were reserved for the aged and infirm, including an elderly patient from the hospital who had been carried in on a stretcher. The gymnasium had been opened to the public. The place was a madhouse of confusion. Excited small children screamed or wept, while older ones ran through the crowd, yelling and playing with basketballs. Chairs around the edge of the large room were occupied by women stunned to silence, contemplating the possible destruction of their homes.

The night was chilly but clear. The stars appeared cold and remote, unaffected by Alaska's distress. I found a place outdoors, sheltered from the wind, where I could sit and watch the harbor and listen to my radio. People moved restlessly in and out of the gymnasium, probably feeling as helpless as I did.

Many of the boat owners had gone to the harbor, trying to decide what to do. Some of the captains of larger boats had already headed out, knowing the boats would be safer riding out a tidal wave in the open waters of the lower Cook Inlet than if caught in the confined boat harbor. None of the men from the birthday party had come to the school, and the women looked after their children alone.

Some of the elderly men at the school plodded down the

hill occasionally, to see what was happening at the water's edge. The tide was ebbing and nearly low. Then it started flooding fast

The tsunami was attacking the central coast of Alaska, and we heard the disastrous reports. One Kodiak crab boat skipper described a parade of wreckage drifting through the channel and out to sea from the devastated Kodiak waterfront. He and other boat operators who had headed for deep water at the first tsunami warning watched in amazement as small buildings, fishing boats, an entire fish cannery that had been built on a scow before being jacked up on pilings, came floating out on the calm seas.

The crab boat skipper reported his crew in a bit of quandary: They could see a waterfront liquor store drifting upright nearby, as well as an amphibious plane that had been lifted off its ramp on the waterfront. The crew was debating, he said, whether to take the plane in tow or salvage the contents of the liquor store.

Later we heard the Wakefield Fisheries plant at Port Wakefield try to contact one of the fishermen tied up at the boat harbor in Kodiak. When the boat finally answered, the radio operator asked for its location.

"I'm up in the schoolyard, a thousand feet from the harbor," the skipper replied.

His boat had been caught on the crest of the wave and carried over what had been the main part of Kodiak. It was stranded by the receding water with little damage to boat or crew.

The fishing boats tied up in Seldovia's boat harbor initially bore the brunt of the local earthquake damage. Many of them were small salmon seiners and drift boats tied up at the boat float, their engines drained and laid up for the winter. While the larger crab boats steamed out of the harbor to safer waters, the little boats could not readily be started.

Their owners struggled desperately for an engine spark while the water flooded into the boat harbor.

The entrance between the two rock jetties was plugged by a torrent that crested and foamed as it forced its way into the boat basin. Wood screamed against wood as the boat floats sawed against the upright pilings that moored them in place. The water boiled with eddies and whirlpools that engulfed the boat basin.

Water pressure was so great that the floats and the boats tied to them could not withstand it. A large shrimp boat wrenched loose and dragged tons of debris with it. The pilings broke off with sounds like gunshots, and the 10-inch-square timbers that supported the floats in long walkways splintered into short sections. Floats, fishing boats and broken pilings all were adrift in a mass of rubble.

As the inrushing water met the resisting land at the head of the harbor it was deflected. Some of the water backed up the slough, flooding the banks and swamping part of the airfield. The bulk of the flood, turned aside by the resisting land and the narrow throat of the slough, formed a gigantic whirlpool, contained by the shore and the rock jetties that formed the boat basin. Fishing boats, the broken floats and timbers, all the debris carried by the flood were caught in the maelstrom and commenced a stately circling.

The movement braided all the wreckage together. Those men who were still on their boats fended off wreckage with pike poles, fought against tie-up lines, or continued to labor over balky engines in an effort to escape.

As the flood drained back into the wider Seldovia Bay, the circling movement slowed and the wreckage loosened. Masses of debris were stranded high up on the embankments along with the big shrimp boat. Finally the men could untangle their boats. With all the force, movement and terror, it seemed a miracle that no one was injured or killed.

144

On the schoolhouse hill we learned only snatches of what was happening in the harbor. As I sat in the darkness listening to the radio, I worried about Ted. The *Alaska Standard* had been in Seldovia a few days earlier, and the next destination was Cordova. I tried to quell my fears by deciding the tanker was under way in open waters and would easily ride out the tsunami unharmed. With all the chatter on the air, I heard no word of Valdez or Seward. Anchorage sounded chaotic, with streets collapsed, fires raging, buildings crumbling, people missing, whole neighborhoods barred from public access.

Some of us in Seldovia thought we were one of the few waterfront communities in the North Pacific to be spared. The water had flooded to the edge of the boardwalk, but the plank and timber structure escaped damage. When nothing else happened and Seldovia seemed safe, people straggled back home. The Seldovia waterfront was saved because the surge of water had come at low tide. Had the tide been high, the boardwalk, the processing plants, stores, taverns and all other structures built at the water's edge would have been swamped and washed away.

A few townsfolk who lived near the edge of the harbor decided to stay overnight at the school. Most other residents, I among them, decided to trust to an all-night watchman to sound the alarm if danger threatened again.

Early the next morning as I walked to work, only a few signs of the hectic night remained. The beaches were littered with tidal wave debris, but the waterfront buildings and boardwalk showed no signs of damage. The boat basin, only recently constructed, enclosed a mass of wreckage, but some of the fishing captains were already rounding up the floats that had been cast adrift. A few of the mooring pilings still stood erect or leaning, and men labored to tie the damaged floats together to make some jury-rigged place to tie the boats.

As I passed one of the taverns, Ray Blackett, son of the owner, came out to intercept me. He had a short-wave radio station set up in the building and kept schedules with many boats and ships in the North Pacific. During the night he had talked to the *Alaska Standard* and had a message for me. The ship had been caught at the dock in Seward when the tsunami hit there. The tanker escaped but Ted was injured. As far as Ray understood, Ted's legs had been broken and he was left behind in the Seward Hospital.

By this time some news of the extent of the damage wrought by the quake was trickling into Seldovia, mostly by short-wave radio from boats and fish plants in distant areas. Seward was one of the places severely damaged.

I guessed that the Seward Hospital must be crowded with casualties. Dr. Osric Armstrong, who was Seldovia's doctor at that time, told me that if I could get Ted to Seldovia, he could be cared for in our hospital. I called the state trooper in Homer by radio and asked him to get in touch with Ted's brother in Sterling. I was sure Walt would fly to Seward and bring Ted to Seldovia.

Anxiously I awaited news, and when I had not heard from Walt by midafternoon I chartered the local air taxi operator to fly me to Seward. We had not gone far when we sighted many earthquake signs. The fairly flat land north of the Homer bluffs was broken into waves created in the snow. Tustumena Lake surface ice had been shattered into large, symmetrical floes, each rimmed with black on all edges by the mud that was forced up from the lake bottom and squeezed through the cracks in the ice.

As we entered Resurrection Pass we saw gigantic bare spots and enormous heaps of fresh rock piles, where landslides had roared down the mountainsides. The damage was awesome, further indication of the forces that had shaken Alaska the previous evening.

Resurrection Pass was alive with military planes darting to and from Seward like swarms of bees. When we landed at the airstrip an officious local authority ran toward us, screaming and waving his arms.

"Take off! Get away! This airfield is closed. We don't want any sightseers."

He wouldn't listen to us try to explain our mission. The pilot had made ready to take off when another man ran toward us. He was a Seward volunteer fireman and a commercial fisherman who recognized me. He told me Walt had been there earlier and hiked to the hospital in town, only to learn that Ted had been evacuated to the hospital at Elmendorf Air Force Base outside Anchorage. Walt assumed that word of this had been sent to me, so he did not try to call me.

No further message came from or about Ted. For several days after returning to Seldovia I did not know what had happened to him or where he might be now. My guess was that he had been sent on to the Marine Hospital in Seattle.

Finally one morning he called me. He was in Homer, waiting for the weather to clear so he could come to Seldovia. The Air Force doctor had wanted to send him to the Marine Hospital but Ted refused to go. With his legs in casts, he had been given a pair of crutches and released from the Air Force hospital. He made his own way to Homer by commercial flight.

The fine weather over the Easter weekend had turned to snow. Planes were grounded. Ted was stuck in Homer for the day. Just before dark he called again and told me he was in pain and would check into the Homer Hospital for the night. He would try to come to Seldovia the next day.

The doctor in Homer would not release him. Ted was in worse shape than he realized. Although only the smaller tibia bones in his legs were broken, he should not have been walking around. His legs had swollen after the casts were put on at Elmendorf. The first thing the Homer doctor had done was to cut off the casts.

As soon as the weather cleared, I flew to Homer to see Ted. His legs were terribly swollen, as though the skin might burst and peel away. They were all colors from black to blue and a yellow, liverish shade. He had a bad cut on his head, his only other injury. Although he had been sedated he seemed keyed up and more than usually voluble.

The doctor warned me privately that Ted might suffer psychological effects from his terrible ordeal. He had gone through an amazing experience that could not rationally be explained. It was almost too much to believe but was corroborated by his shipmates when I talked to them later.

The *Alaska Standard* had been tied to the Seward petroleum dock that earthquake afternoon. The tanker's job was to distribute fuel to smaller ports in western Alaska, and it was taking on several kinds of petroleum products through heavy hoses running between ship and shore. Ted was on dock watch, pacing back and forth, making sure all the hoses and valves were functioning properly, when he felt the dock shiver under his feet. Then the dock warehouse creaked and screeched as the sheets of corrugated iron siding on the building chafed together.

"Earthquake!" he yelled to the man on watch on the tanker deck.

The dock began to heave and pitch.

"Get aboard, Ted!" his shipmate shouted.

Ted ran to the ship's ladder. The tanker rolled violently. No way could Ted climb to the deck. He turned to run ashore. The fuel lines ruptured. Flammable fuel sprayed into the air like glittering fountains as the hose connections pulled apart. At any moment the fuel might ignite. Ted dared not run through it. As he turned back to the tanker he felt the dock disintegrate under his feet. He sank into the water, felt a blow on his head, and remembered nothing more.

By rare good fortune the engine crew had remained on board while the tanker was reloading, and the captain was in the pilothouse. The engines were silent, as they always were when cargo was being handled. As the tsunami surged against the ship, the engineer started the engines instantly upon the captain's command. Moments later, with the tie-up lines and loading hoses trailing, the tanker headed full-speed into deeper waters, leaving several crewmen behind on shore.

The next thing Ted knew, he was getting to his feet. All around him lay boards, timbers, pieces of corrugated iron siding that had been part of the dock and warehouse. He stared around and saw the *Alaska Standard* wheelhouse, with no idea how he had reached the ship. He grabbed the mast to steady himself as the tanker headed away from shore to anchor in the middle of Resurrection Bay.

His shipmates could hardly believe it when they saw Ted crawl out of the rubble on deck. The last they had seen of him was as he disappeared in the collapse of the dock. They had seen the backwash of the wave sweep over the ship's deck, carrying the ruins of the petroleum dock. In some miraculous way Ted was tangled in that wreckage and left aboard when the sea water drained away.

FIFTEEN

Strains in a Marriage

THE DOCTOR kept Ted in the Homer Hospital for more than a week, then reluctantly discharged him. When Ted arrived in Seldovia he was still keyed up from his experience. I thought he should have gone to Seattle for further treatment. He insisted all he needed was time, to knit the bones in his legs which were now without casts.

There were only two small rooms in the cottage where I had been living, the kitchen and the living-bedroom with a double bed in one corner. I turned this over to Ted and borrowed a cot that I set up in the kitchen for myself.

We were very busy in the plant. The company plant at Port Wakefield had been so badly damaged by the tsunami that it had to be abandoned. The large boats that fished in

151

Aleutian waters and customarily delivered their catch to Port Wakefield now brought their loads of king crab to Seldovia to be processed. This meant daily plant operation and even overtime.

It seemed to me that Ted and I had always been happier together when on the homestead. Especially in the first few years, we shared dreams, plans and ambitions. In town, whether in Seldovia or Seward, he was usually on vacation from his job whenever we were together, while my life was dominated by daily office responsibilities. This interfered with his conviction that he should be the center of my activities, and caused tension between us. After the quake I remembered the Homer doctor's warning that Ted might suffer psychological damage from what had happened to him, and tried to make allowances for his demands.

Before and after office work I looked after him and did the extra cooking, laundry and entertaining he expected. He disliked the place where I lived and kept pointing out flaws that could not easily be remedied. No other houses were available for rent and I tried to persuade him to make the best of it until we could move back home. Ironically, the house was more comfortable for me than the Bear Cove cabin. At least it provided running water, an inside bathroom and oil heat, so I did not have to carry water and gather firewood.

We had extremely high tides twice a month that hampered plant production, as the harbor waters came up to the dock and sometimes overflowed it. The explanation given us for this unusual flooding was that the tides were erratic as an aftermath of the earthquake but would soon settle back to normal. Since we still had frequent aftershocks, the explanation was plausible.

While I was at the office every day, Ted had a lot of company. When word of his experience got out, his fishing grounds acquaintances came to hear his story at first hand. Within a few weeks he was able to get around on crutches and began thinking of the time when he could go back to work. When the *Alaska Standard* came to port, one of the mates told me the company had plans for Ted, and we guessed a promotion was in the offing. Ted was a licensed mate through his experience on his father's trading ship, qualified to advance from deckhand.

A short time before he planned to leave for Seattle to prepare for getting back to work, a boat mishap occurred outside Seldovia. A two-man crab boat coming across the Inlet from the west side began taking on water and started to sink. The captain called for help, giving his location, and other boats sped to his rescue. The two men were saved and brought back to Seldovia.

While to me this was a fairly common incident, Ted was violently affected. He demanded that I go to the harbor to meet the rescue boat and interview the shipwrecked seamen for a report to the *Anchorage Daily Times.* I had already learned by experience that local happenings were of no great interest to the city editors and that this did not warrant a story, except as an item in my weekly column. Perhaps Ted equated the fishermen's narrow escape with his own experience and thought I was making light of it. At any rate, he stormed out of the house on his crutches and limped along the boardwalk toward the center of town.

To appease him I did go to the boat harbor, interviewed the shipwrecked fishermen, then went to the office to write up the story and telephone it to Anchorage. Two days later a few lines appeared in the *Times,* not my detailed story but a brief item sent in by a man in Homer.

We quarreled that night and in the morning there was no truce between us. I was weary of my double life, on one hand a successful writer and productive worker, on the other a submissive, self-effacing wife. In the past few years my life-long low self-esteem had gradually risen and I was no longer willing to be completely dominated as I had been, first by my father, then by my husband. Our lives together had gone terribly wrong and I did not know how to repair the situation.

When I got home for lunch that day, Ted was gone. As far as I could see, he had taken all his clothes and other belongings. After a few inquiries that afternoon, I learned he had hired someone to take him to Bear Cove. I assumed he would go directly to Seattle from there and we would not meet again. The next evening I told Candy Hendrix that our marriage was probably at an end.

I was mistaken. A few days later Ted returned, but only briefly. We were cold to each other. We did not quarrel again, but the bitter words we had exchanged earlier seemed to hang in the air between us.

After all the years we had been together and all we had gone through, I was still not willing to initiate a break, and apparently he felt the same way. He left for Seattle for out-patient therapy and to take a course in Loran navigation so he could qualify as mate on the *Alaska Standard*. We corresponded in a distant way, and I still hoped that somehow we could achieve a kind of harmony.

SIXTEEN

'Wall-to-Wall Seawater'

OUR PERSONAL problems were overshadowed by the problems of Seldovia. The euphoria of being spared from devastation by the Good Friday earthquake began to fade. When we heard of the destruction of the Kodiak, Seward and Valdez waterfronts we were even more grateful for the comparatively minor damage we had suffered. But as time went on, we were not so sure.

The tides did not settle back to normal as everyone had predicted. Instead, every month at the peak of the tidal cycle the town's waterfront was awash. At least once a month the water covered the floors of the stores, the warehouses and the seafood plants. Our plant engineer had to barricade the compressor room with sandbags to keep salt water from seeping in and damaging the equipment. The Wakefield dock was awash at high water, as were the low spots in the processing plant.

"I'm tired of wall-to-wall seawater," one store owner moaned as she swept the tidal water out after the usual monthly flood.

The boardwalk was the main problem. Parts of it flooded on every high tide. If it should lift and then settle askew, the main street would be wiped out. While automobiles and people on foot could use the back roads, with the boardwalk gone there would be no way to move the salmon, shrimp, king crab and halibut pack to the city dock for shipment, or stove oil to the buildings on the waterfront.

The Army Engineers brought sandbags which local people filled and placed along the edge of the boardwalk to weight it down. Cannery and private docks were also weighted down to secure them, while a few people still insisted that, given time, the tides would go back to normal.

Others began to believe that the land had dropped as a result of the earthquake. Salmon fishermen reported that all along the shores of the southern Kenai Peninsula spruce trees were dying, since their roots and sometimes lower branches were immersed in salt water. The trees along the shores of Kachemak Bay, including Green Timbers campground on Homer Spit, were also turning brown. Word spread that the town of Portage at the head of Turnagain Arm had dropped so much that the entire townsite had to be abandoned. And at Hope, what had been broad tide flats usually above the waters of Turnagain Arm were now under water most of the time.

I remembered what friends had told me about the Sacramento River delta in California when we had lived at Roe

Island Light Station. Before the San Francisco earthquake in 1906 the islands had been farmland, well above the reach of the highest tides. After the earthquake some of the islands sank completely out of sight, while other parts were cut by sloughs and ditches and the dry land became swampy. Island farms were ruined and abandoned; some of the buildings were moved away or raised on pilings and converted to duck hunting clubs. I began to fear a similar land drop had occurred at Seldovia.

The largest tides of the year were due in late autumn. By now everyone in town knew that we were in for trouble. More sandbags were placed the entire length of the boardwalk. Heavy equipment was trundled out on all the docks to weight them down. In the waterfront stores and their warehouses, case goods and sacks of flour and sugar were placed high up on racks and counters, preparing for a flood.

Soon after the earthquake, the Salvation Army had sent officers to Seldovia to offer whatever assistance was needed. Every kid in town soon sported a shiny new jacket as a goodwill token. More substantially, the Salvation Army brought in a house-moving outfit that jacked up every flooded waterfront residence at the owner's request. Some declined but others accepted the help, and 10 or 12 dwellings were raised.

These raised homes were not endangered by the threat of flood in autumn, but others now prepared for the worst. It appeared that the entire population of Seldovia roamed the boardwalk and docks as the hour of high tide approached. Newspaper and radio reporters came down from Anchorage for the spectacular event.

Nothing very exciting happened that month. The tide came up quietly, flooded the boardwalk and waterfront buildings, and as quietly ebbed without doing much damage. The outsiders left, disappointed, while residents waited for the next series of tides a month later, which as always in autumn would also be extremely high.

This time Seldovia's slow water torture came to a climax. A southwest gale brought six inches of snow. At the peak of the tides the gale continued, causing the back-up of North Pacific waters in Cook Inlet. The tides, already unnaturally high, were increased by the late autumn storm.

The tide poured relentlessly into Seldovia Bay. The slough overflowed, flooding the end of the airstrip and softening the rest of it. The low spots on the road to the cemetery and the Outside Beach were under water for several hours, marooning those who lived out of town.

Houses on the shore side of the boardwalk, unaffected by previous high tides, were now awash. In the Seldovia House hotel, salt water poured over the top of the bathtub and toilet. A warehouse perched on spindly pilings on Watch Point collapsed and went adrift, threatening to crash into the city dock, which was nearly under water.

The Wakefield Fisheries plant was also in danger. Some of the pilings were rotten, and because the plant had been added onto at different times the main timbers were unconnected. The large live-tanks in the plant had been pumped full of water to add weight if the tidewater rose above the dock. Expecting that the entire building might collapse, we moved out all the office books and other records.

The water crept through the plant and to the bottom of the compressor room windows on the shore side of the boardwalk. In the mess hall, seawater backed up in the floor drains and flooded the whole room and the old cannery office. Though the flood surrounded the freezer building, the airtight doors kept it outside. At high tide one of the plant foremen rowed a skiff from the dock through the entire plant and to the mess hall door on the usually dry side of the boardwalk.

After that experience no one could doubt that Seldovia had problems. The waterfront had ultimately been destroyed as surely as if it had been washed away on the night of the earthquake.

FROM THE time Ted had left for Seattle our letters were guarded and cool. After a month in Seattle he had gone back on the *Alaska Standard* as one of the mates. We kept in touch but my feelings toward him were noncommittal. I decided to take vacation time from my job and go to New York in the fall to confer with my agent and editors, none of whom I had ever met.

But I reflected that if I did that, our lives would probably separate completely. Our interests were already in different directions, and if I seriously pursued and expanded my literary ambitions, our marriage was probably over. I was not yet ready for such a drastic step.

Ted seemed happier and more settled when the tanker came to bring fuel to Seldovia, but he complained of pains in his still unhealed legs. I suggested that we take a trip to Hawaii. The tanker officers spent four months on the ship and then got two months off with pay. I could take an extra month's vacation and we could spend two winter months in a warm climate where he could walk in the sand and swim in the sea to strengthen his legs. He was delighted with my proposal. Apparently he felt as I did, that this trip would also heal the rift between us.

We went to Maui, to a resort I had chosen from a Hawaii Visitors Association brochure. It was a small place, just a few cottages, halfway to Lahaina from the airport. Ted didn't drive and my license had lapsed years before, so we couldn't rent a car. Our landlady, a vivacious Tahitian, drove us around and we had a fine time.

One of our excursions was to watch an international golf tournament on the west side of Maui. I was fascinated by the sight of famous golfers and took photos as we trailed them around the beautiful greens. At one hole I had a clear view of Jack Nicklaus and Arnold Palmer as they played the course together. The announcer had warned the spectators about taking pictures as the players were addressing the ball, and I was determined to wait until Arnold Palmer had made his stroke. He was at the top of his swing when the premature click of my camera shutter sounded like a thunderclap. He whirled, his club still aloft, a look of rage on his face as he confronted me. I thought he was going to lower that club on my head.

People hissed, groaned, yelled at me. I deserved it, and wanted to die. Palmer teed off again and hit his ball with such fury it was one of the tournament's most spectacular shots. While the crowd moved on I stayed behind, wishing I could disappear. A stranger paused and spoke to me.

"Don't feel so bad. He never would have hit a shot like that if you hadn't made him so furious."

The words comforted me a little, but my humiliation was complete when a cartoon of the incident appeared on the front page of the Honolulu newspaper the next morning.

On Christmas Eve, our landlady and her husband invited us to their home for cocktails. They were interested in our life in Alaska and we told them of our experiences. They were particularly fascinated by accounts of tentkeeping and clearing land in the remote wilderness.

Maybe I talked too much. Maybe Ted had too many Mai Tais. He thought I was claiming too much credit for our homestead accomplishments. When we returned to our cottage he snarled at me:

"Whatever you did on the homestead doesn't amount to

one damned thing." His words stunned me into despair. In one cruel sentence he wiped out any pride and attachment I had for our life at Bear Cove.

SEVENTEEN

Seldovia in Turmoil

FOR NEARLY two years, because of the earthquake and my own personal concerns, I wrote almost nothing. Feelings ran so high in Seldovia about how to face and solve community problems that I lost heart and wrote the newspaper columns only intermittently. Although I tried to report objectively, some people took offense at anything that appeared in the newspaper that did not favor their side of the controversy.

When people realized that the Seldovia waterfront had been ruined although it was still in place, three plans of action were considered. The first was for the city to apply for federal funds that had been appropriated through the Alaska State Housing Authority (ASHA) for earthquake damage reconstruction. Seward, Kodiak, Anchorage and Valdez had chosen this route and their projects were already in the planning stage.

The second option was for the town to do its own reconstruction of the boardwalk with pay-as-you-go projects, with businesses, processing plants and individuals responsible for their own repair and reconstruction.

A few people still held out for doing nothing, believing that the tides would eventually go back to normal. This was the third option.

ASHA officials came to explain their program. They would restore all public facilities: rebuild the new but damaged water system, build a sewer system for residents as well as for processing plants, and replace the boardwalk with a solid rock fill. The boat harbor would be enlarged and repaired. The airfield was already being built up and lengthened by a different government agency.

Those people who lived in or had property in the reconstruction area would be bought out by ASHA. Owners had no obligation to rebuild if they chose not to, and were still eligible for low-interest-rate disaster loans to be used anywhere, not only in Seldovia. No repayment was required the first year, interest only for the next four years, with principal payments starting after five years.

Since I had nothing to gain or lose, I personally favored the first plan. I did not give enough attention to the emotional side of the issue and thought complete rebuilding of the waterfront was obviously the best plan for Seldovia's future. I did not understand that some people were willing to put up with regular flooding in order to save Seldovia as it was, until it could be repaired piecemeal.

While the first proposal seemed generous and desirable to many, others objected. The project had no plans to restore the boardwalk and rebuild the waterfront as it had been before the earthquake, but proposed to modernize the town. To many, this was sacrilege. The boardwalk was a symbol of Seldovia. Without it, some people feared, the town would become a nonentity with little distinction, just another jerry-built town.

Others, old-timers as well as newcomers, said "good riddance." The boardwalk had originally been built for foot traffic and for the wheeled tractor that delivered fuel to waterfront establishments and hauled four-wheeled flatbed trucks of freight between processing plants and the city dock.

As automobiles were brought to town, they were at first banned from the boardwalk but gradually took it over. In winter, deep ruts in the snow were filled with water as the snow melted and then froze, making walking slippery and hazardous. In summer, the town's large population of dogs raced along the boardwalk, mostly at night, their droppings a disgusting booby trap for the unwary pedestrian.

Whenever a car drove along the boardwalk, pedestrians had to take refuge in convenient doorways or perch on the railing, depending on their agility. To some people a solid-fill road seemed like a big improvement. For months the controversy raged. Members of the city council were reluctant to impose a decision on the people and decided to call for a non-binding, unofficial public referendum to guide them.

The plant owners and operators got into the argument, all of them urging acceptance of the ASHA project. Wakefield Fisheries was already building a new Kodiak area plant and intended to do the same in Seldovia. The salmon cannery management posted signs around town promising to rebuild in Seldovia if the project was accepted, but to move their operations to Port Graham if the vote went the other way. The fishermen trusted the cannery operator, and some were influenced by the promises. The referendum on accepting the ASHA plan passed by a decisive majority.

In the end, the ASHA project was accepted and the council signed the agreement. A score or more families moved away, some to Kodiak, some to Homer and some Outside. Others who remained were intensely bitter, and the town was divided by disharmony.

Appraisers came in and set prices on waterfront property. Some people were satisfied and sold out right away. Others were dissatisfied but in the interest of getting the rebuilding started accepted what they felt was a niggardly offer. Still others were outraged, refused to sign and eventually filed suit for a more favorable appraisal. When they won, those who had already sold felt betrayed by their public-spiritedness.

Despite the promises, the salmon and shrimp cannery owners took their money and ran, one to Port Graham, the other to Kodiak. The Alaska Shellfish cannery sold out to ASHA and never rebuilt anywhere. Only Wakefield Fisheries started to build a fine new plant as soon as restored waterfront land became available.

Then came the surveys. Every week, it seemed, a new team came to town to make population, economic, demographic and historical surveys. None of the teams seemed to exchange information, so the same questions were asked over and over and I, at least, couldn't remember from one interview to another what answers I had given. Much of the information requested could only be answered with guesswork, and many of us did not take the interviewers seriously. No one had much prior experience with such a large government project.

It seemed to me that any person in the United States who had ever wanted a trip to Alaska found a government job on some earthquake project or another. Their prior experience, from what I could learn, ranged from managing money market funds for a banking combine to running a vegetable packing cannery in one of the western states to any bureaucratic employment outside Alaska. All these survey and study costs were charged to our project, and I was stunned when the local manager told me a million dollars had been spent before a wheel was ever turned. This sum was about a quarter of the total amount allotted to Seldovia.

The first reconstruction plan presented for council approval was totally unsuitable. Designed by a California firm, it featured parks and uncovered malls on prime waterfront property that would not be usable during six or seven months of bad winter weather, and left little room for the waterfront industries vital to the town's survival. The council rejected that plan, and the wait went on.

Before and during this time, Ted and I had our own problems with the federal government. Ted finally acknowledged we would never be able to clear and cultivate 10 acres of our homestead. We had cleared four acres in addition to the homesite, and planted grass between the stumps. This might qualify us for 32 acres of land, so we applied for that amount.

Our request was rejected. The federal land office stated that since we had filed on 80 acres and had not proved up on that, our claim could not be reduced but was thrown out entirely.

After all the work we had done and the years we had lived on the land, we could not accept this. The fight was left to me. With Ted on the tanker, I started a letter campaign. The disallowment had been made in the Anchorage office. I appealed to Washington and was turned down. I appealed to the Secretary of the Interior and to U.S. Senators Bartlett and Gruening. Later I learned that other people with land claim problems hired attorneys, but this did not occur to me. I fought on, asking anyone who might have any influence to write letters on our behalf. After several years of letter writing, through Senator Gruening our amended claim was finally approved.

The survey was made but the issuance of the deed was held up by the land freeze in connection with the pending Alaska Native Claims Settlement Act. The patents to the 32 acres and the 10-acre cannery site were issued to Ted some time after 1971, when I had already moved away from Bear Cove.

Ted apparently did not realize how deeply wounded I had been by his denunciation of me in Hawaii. In the past, no matter the heat of our quarrels, our relationship went on as before. This time the hurt he had inflicted would not heal, but I hid my feelings from him and from friends and relatives.

My generation of women was marriage oriented, and despite my hurts, both mental and physical, despite the many disappointments, I was not mentally prepared to live a single life. Although we had spent much of the time apart, our marriage was still a fact of my life. As our interests continued to diverge I was glad that we had no family, even though that meant I was completely alone except for Ted.

Our relationship became one of uninvolved acquaintance. When the tanker brought fuel to Seldovia, we visited for a few hours and he invited fellow officers to join us in my apartment. He spent his summer leaves at Bear Cove, or salvaging lumber in Seldovia as the waterfront buildings were demolished, while I remained on my job. In the winters we made two more trips to Hawaii and spent one leave in Seattle. He never met my family except when my brother and sister visited Alaska. Our attitude on our trips was as though we were unrelated fellow travelers on a cruise, spending at least half of the time apart.

Almost two years after the time of the earthquake I wrote

another book. *The Mystery of Kama Lu* was my least successful book and indicated that my main audience was in Alaska or those interested in Alaska. With a Hawaiian background, and my name unknown in that context, *Kama Lu* sold only 2,000 copies. Reprint rights were sold to a Portuguese publisher, but I don't know whether that edition was printed.

In Seldovia, the construction part of the urban renewal project finally started. For years the town was in turmoil. Even ardent project proponents were dismayed at the ways money was spent. If they had had a choice, many who had initially favored the project would have voted to call the whole thing off. It was too late for that.

We watched the boardwalk sawed in sections, loaded on trucks and carted away. We saw waterfront buildings demolished, the wreckage burned. We were battered by the clatter of air hammers as dynamite holes were drilled in the cliffs near the waterfront, to blast them away. Cap's Hill in the center of town was broken up and leveled to provide rock fill material for the waterfront road that replaced the boardwalk.

The processing plants, the stores, hotel, old schoolhouse and all the old residences in the project area were demolished. Mobile homes were brought in to house the displaced who were unable to find housing elsewhere. Residents were welcome to salvage what they could in the project area before the wrecking crew took over, but few chose to do so.

Seldovia was like a battlefield. In our little town, lifelong friendships were broken. Some people came to hate me for the articles I wrote about the project. I had had tunnel vision, focused as I was on the project benefits, with not enough empathy for the possible sufferings of the uprooted. After many years the subject is still an emotional one, particularly with those who had known Seldovia before World War II.

When the project was finished, Seldovia assumed an entirely new character. Where Cap's Hill had been, the center of town was a wide, gravel-based bare expanse divided into small building lots that were not sold for years. The new Wakefield Fisheries plant was on one end of the waterfront, closer to Watch Point and to the mouth of the harbor. A new city dock and warehouses were built near the processing plant. The new boat harbor was larger and deeper to accommodate the big crab boats that had been added to the salmon boat fleet. The waterfront property was zoned commercial and was not occupied for a number of years, with a very few exceptions.

Only one grocery store was rebuilt, a large metal building also housing a Laundromat and a tavern, with apartments upstairs. The Linwood Bar was rebuilt but the Surf Club and the Polar Bar were gone forever. Jack and Susan English built a new building, part of which was leased to the federal government for a new post office. Pete Polson built a beautiful theater that was later forced out of business by the advent of television in Seldovia. It is now mostly shops, apartments and warehouse space.

These few reconstructions were not enough to make Seldovia the vibrant little seaport it once had been. With no mailboats any more, and no freight or passenger vessels, the only regular boat service was the state ferry that also served Seward, Kodiak and Homer. The town enjoyed a few years of prosperity as the king crab fishery came to a climax. When it crashed, Seldovia was almost dormant. A logging venture in Kachemak Bay brought income for a while, since the loggers and their families lived in Seldovia. A road that was built to the sawmill and logging area now provides access to the

Seldovia Native Association subdivision, and to Rocky Bay on the south end of the Kenai Peninsula.

In recent years Seldovia has turned into a resort town. Many new homes have been built and old ones renovated or torn down, purchased mainly for the waterfront location. When the crab and shrimp fisheries crashed, the former Wakefield plant changed ownership several times and now operates only intermittently. Large crab boats no longer operate out of the little port, and many of the smaller boat operators fish for Homer processing plants, where they find a steadier market for salmon and shellfish.

Summers are lively, but the town population is divided between permanent residents and summer people, with the balance slowly tipping to part-time newcomers. The large bare flat that was the Cap's Hill area has been almost completely rebuilt, first by highliner crab fishermen during the prosperous years, and now by summer residents. Old-timers mourn that Seldovia is ruined. Still, the harbor is as beautiful as it ever was, the surrounding mountains loom protectively, and more houses have been built in the outlying areas. To those who don't hark back to the past, it is still a charming and friendly place.

While all this was happening to Seldovia, my life was also changing. After the Hawaii book I wanted to try something different. There was a story in the Alaska earthquake and its ramifications, but with so many conditions still unsettled, the right time for a book had not come. In the meantime I decided to write a nonfiction book. My agent arranged a contract with Coward McCann Publishers for me to write the *Alaska* volume for their States of the Nation series.

This was the first time I had worked under close supervision of an editor. At first I didn't like it. I would write a chapter and send it to her. She read and returned it with comments and suggestions. She had a little trouble with Alaska terms. One of her questions was, "What do you mean by *treed* by a moose?"

I had to do a lot of research as well as call on my own experiences. I made trips, flying to Fairbanks and Kodiak and traveling to Southeast Alaska on the state ferry system. My horizons were broadened, and homestead life sank deeper into the past.

For the last two years in Seldovia I had a comfortable, modern place to live, in one of the apartments over the new grocery store. I settled down to an almost cloistered life. The Hendrixes had left Seldovia when Chuck was promoted to assistant to the president of the company. Most of my social life had revolved around them, and now I rarely went out in the evenings except to Hospital Guild meetings. Every morning I was at my typewriter no later than six o'clock, after a first cup of coffee, working on a manuscript.

As soon as I finished the Alaska book I started writing *House Upon a Rock*. This was my earthquake book, the story of a family living in a town that was a composite of Seldovia, Seward and Kodiak. It portrayed the tragedy created by the earthquake and told how the people met their troubles and survived. Like *Fisherman's Choice*, the new book was a Junior Literary Guild selection and also sold out two editions published by Atheneum Publishers.

In the following year, *Petticoat Fisherman*, the story of a girl working on her father's crab fishing boat, was the last book of mine published by Atheneum. Ives Washburn published another book for younger children, *The Mystery of the Alaska Queen*. Neither book sold very well. Although all my books, totaling 13, were still in print, I had an uneasy feeling about my writing.

For his part, Ted was getting restless. Shipboard life was

palling on him and he wanted to come ashore. When I made a tentative suggestion that we settle in Homer, for I knew he disliked Seldovia, he would not hear of it. Bear Cove was his home and he wanted no other.

In truth, my contentment in Seldovia also had dimmed. The urban renewal controversy had left its scars, and I was disillusioned by all the aftermath of ill feelings. The atmosphere at the crab plant was also different. Instead of the warm, comfortable feeling among the employees at the old plant, in the new establishment, with new management, the relationships were impersonal. An atmosphere of competitiveness among the executives replaced the feeling almost of kinship we had during the Hendrix years.

Sadly, after years of faithful service it was with a bitter feeling that I left Wakefield Fisheries to go back to Bear Cove. Despite the fact that the auditor who inspected our books annually had told me I kept the best company records and required the least corrections of any of the Alaska plants, I learned that I was the lowest paid bookkeeper in the organization. The owner admitted this but excused it because I was now the only woman bookkeeper. He told my superintendent that to make up for the inequity I would be given a substantial bonus when I left, but this did not happen.

The man who replaced me was hired at $100 a month more than my ending salary. On the day I left he got into a drunken brawl, was fired and left town the same day. His replacement could not keep up the work, and a woman was hired to assist him. With no equal rights law at that time, I had no recourse but resignation and resentment.

EIGHTEEN

Return to Bear Cove

BEAR Cove seemed peaceful after the life we had led for the previous six years. We returned home in July, when natural conditions were at their best. It was 24 years to the month since our first arrival, and as we settled in I had hopes that this time life would be better.

The serenity, the isolation, the myriad of waterfowl, the beauty of the surroundings, all contributed to my initial sense of optimism. While I busied myself getting settled in the cabin, Ted started to work on the projects he had planned while we were away.

We did have problems. The land drop that affected much of southcentral Alaska had also occurred at Bear Cove. Our warehouse that Ted had built well above even the highest tides was now flooded every month. All the tools and equipment on the floor had been ruined in the original tsunami. On his summer leaves Ted had put everything up on benches and pallets, but after our return it seemed that every month we forgot and left something on the floor, to be caught by the flooding tide.

What was more disappointing was that the warehouse had been broken into during our absence. Ted had nailed the front and back doors shut, so that although a boat could tie up to the dock the boatmen could not go into the warehouse or get ashore from the dock. We learned that two men had tied up to the dock, planning to head over the ridge with some bulky equipment. They broke the warehouse doors open so they could unload their freight on the dock and carry it through the warehouse to shore. They had not bothered to secure the warehouse again.

With the place standing open, passersby had looted as they had also looted the fox farm warehouse. We lost outboard motors, tools and building materials. Fortunately Ted had stored his power tools and chain saws in the cabin. Although an attempt had been made to break in there, it was not successful. We never found out who had robbed us.

No one else lived on our side of Kachemak Bay when we returned. The Kuzma place on Bear Island now belonged to people in Homer who used it only occasionally. Another summer place had been built on the island by John and Phyllis Cooper of Homer, who came up on summer weekends with their two young boys. Bill Eklof's place had an absentee owner, too. The old fox farm was abandoned, a sad sight with the house burned down and Paddy's cabin vandalized. The old man who had repossessed the place returned one summer to restore it, with very little success. The Newman homestead was occasionally used by transients. Pom and Roxy had moved to Anchorage and no one lived at their old home except intermittently. We were more solitary than we had been when we settled at Bear Cove.

The people who came wandering into the Cove around this time in search of a place to live were generally not reassuring. Unlike earlier would-be homesteaders, they were looking for vacant cabins and were not bothered by the fact that they were trespassers. Most of them had unrealistic ideas about living in the wilderness, and no real intention of remaining.

But because we were the only ones living at the Cove, we did get more visitors than in earlier times. Where the fox farm had once been the anchoring place, now people who were headed farther up the bay made our place a waystop. I was always glad to have company, for what once seemed a peaceful and tranquil life had become a lonely one for me, and I welcomed every visitor.

The adventure of 20 years before now felt like pointless drudgery. At 30, carrying water, bathing in a tin washtub and using an outdoor privy were pioneering necessities. In my 50s I found that these primitive arrangements had lost their charm.

In Seldovia I had met a woman who went through the bombing destruction of her European home city during World War II. She knew from experience what I was talking about when describing primitive living.

"I don't agree with that kind of life," she told me flatly. "When plumbing was invented, it was meant to be used."

After Ted's assessment of my land-clearing and other homestead labor, I did very little work outdoors, except around the yard. I was no longer always steady on my feet and sometimes had bad falls, especially when the paths were icy. The place had become Ted's homestead in my mind, and I no longer had any desire to improve it. My interest was only in a flower garden in front of the cabin. I carried rocks and small boulders for a retaining wall and refused his offers of assistance. To me this work was therapy and exercise and I wanted to do it myself.

After moose, sheep and waterfowl hunting seasons closed, upper Kachemak Bay was deserted by visitors. I dreaded winter. We lived like middle-aged brother and sister, together for mutual convenience but with no intimacy between us.

Although I wrote steadily, none of my work was accepted. In many ways my life seemed to be over, but I was not yet willing to concede defeat.

Ted spent his time working on the land and struggling with our major problem, which was access to the cabin from the beach. Years before, he had built a sturdy three-flight stairway up the embankment between the warehouse and the cabin. This served us well for several years. Then an unusually rainy autumn saturated the embankment and the cleared land behind it. The bank collapsed and slid to the beach, carrying the stairway with it.

The trail we then made glaciered over and was useless for most of the winter. Ted turned to the small gully between the cabin and the unfinished house, and tried to build an access road there. He rigged up the heavy hose he had brought from Port Vita and sluiced the earth and rocks away. Although this provided a narrow, steep trail, it was an unsatisfactory solution and he talked of building another stairway.

In spite of all the money we had put into the boat, we still did not have our own transportation. Ted had the boat hauled out in Seldovia and never tried to launch it after he left the tanker. I believe he realized what a mistake the boat had been and therefore put it completely out of his mind.

Despite my lack of success in writing, my book royalties amounted to nearly four thousand dollars in 1969. I decided to write a book for young people about Utah pioneer life and to make a research trip to Salt Lake City. Pioneering was a subject I knew well, and growing up in Salt Lake I had studied Utah history. The need for further research provided an excuse to visit my old home.

This was also a chance to escape Bear Cove for the worst part of the winter. Ted had no objections. Even after the cold and snow ended his outdoor work, we were living separate lives. He had taken over the new "half house" and spent his days there while I remained in the cabin. I did not know what he did all day, and he did not volunteer any information.

My research trip Outside was not quite as I had planned. Soon after I arrived in Salt Lake, my sister telephoned from Tahoe City, California. Her husband had been stricken with a ruptured appendix, requiring major surgery and a long, perilous convalescence. Could I come and help her operate their food concession at Alpine Meadows Ski Resort?

I stayed with them until the heaviest part of the ski season was over, then returned to Salt Lake. After a few weeks of research, the stomach pains I'd experienced for several years drove me to a medical clinic. A doctor in Seattle had told me two years earlier that I probably had ulcers. A more thorough examination in Salt Lake revealed gallstones and possible bile duct obstruction. The same day I learned that, I had an eye examination and the ophthalmologist found cataracts in both eyes.

Surgery took care of my abdominal problems, and the eye doctor advised waiting for the cataracts to develop further. I returned to my sister's home in California where her husband and I convalesced together. Then I went home to Bear Cove, energized and eager to start another book, although because Ted had one wall torn out of the cabin in his latest remodeling efforts it was another six weeks before the place was in shape for concentration.

My agent liked the new book but couldn't place it with a publisher. For the first time I learned how lucky I had been to have all the earlier books accepted. During the 1960s, after I started writing books, the federal government funded a number of cultural programs. One of these helped public and school libraries to buy new books. With increased demand, the publishers increased their juvenile lists dramatically, since libraries are the main market for books for young people. I was a beneficiary; my publishers had a sure market and were willing to take a chance on books by previously unknown writers.

A new federal administration in 1968 curtailed cultural programs, and liberal federal library funds dwindled. Added to this, the lifestyle upheavals of the era also affected young peoples' reading habits. Many of the nation's public libraries are in the larger cities and young people in cities, those who read, did not relate to Alaska. With limited funds, librarians now ordered books more relevant to young people with problems unknown to me or to the characters in my books.

While my writing career seemed to be waning, Ted's life took an unexpected upward turn. With so many freighters from Asia coming into Alaska waters to pick up fishery products every summer and autumn, new state maritime regulations were formulated. These required all large vessels using Alaska ports to carry a licensed marine pilot to command the ship to the dock and out again after the cargo was discharged or loaded. A group of retired Standard Oil Company tanker officers formed a marine pilots association. With Ted's familiarity with Aleutian ports where many of the fish processing plants were located, gained through his experience on the mailboat and the *Alaska Standard,* he was invited to become the Westward pilot.

When a freighter was due to enter a western Alaska harbor, Ted would be summoned by radio from Homer. He flew to Kodiak, Anchorage, Dutch Harbor or whatever airfield was nearest the freighter's destination, and was taken by a pilot boat out to the vessel waiting to enter the port. He brought the ship to the dock and waited aboard while the cargo was loaded, or visited ashore if he happened to have local acquaintances. When the ship was loaded he piloted it out of the harbor and was picked up by the pilot boat and returned to shore.

Although he spoke no foreign language, Ted was an excellent pantomime and mimic and managed very well with his assignments. The ships from Asia usually had at least one officer who knew a few words of English. With this assistance, the flash cards used by international travelers, and pantomime, Ted managed to communicate. He really enjoyed these missions. To me, the most interesting and enviable of his jobs was to pilot Jacques Cousteau's *Calypso* from Anchorage to lower Cook Inlet after the crew had spent a season filming sea otters in the Aleutian Islands. Ted came home with French mannerisms and accent and a fund of new stories about this experience.

The piloting work paid fabulously well. In the first year of our retirement we had had to cash some of my savings bonds, and I worried what would happen when all our savings were spent. Ted's earnings now provided all our money needs and gave him the stimulation of getting away from the homestead occasionally, and doing important and skilled work.

I had worked hard on my Utah book and felt it was some of my best writing. My agent sent it to various publishers and always it was rejected. I had faith in the plot and background, and decided to rewrite, making it into a novel with a young woman instead of a boy as the central character. It was rejected again. By this time I was desperate. I wrote a sequel to *House Upon A Rock,* introducing contemporary characters and problems. The editor of Atheneum Publishers rejected it with the note "I don't think Elsa Pedersen can write for us any more."

The following summer of 1970 was more lively than the two previous years. The state land around Bear Cove was opened to homesite entry and we had a miniature land rush. Although the opening was not advertised, State of Alaska employees learned of it and most of the applicants were employees of the state Fish and Game Department and their friends. Many stopped at our place for directions and those who attempted settlement often came to our cabin to send messages to Homer by radio.

Ted's brother, Walt, stopped by more frequently. He was doing a job of erosion control and seismic trail repair in the Caribou Hills, on the moose range beyond the head of Kachemak Bay. Sometimes when he flew down from Moose River he would find fog over the lake where he usually landed in his float plane and then hiked to the job site. If he couldn't land at the lake he would come on to Bear Cove for a cup of coffee and a visit before making another attempt to reach the Caribou Hills.

Another break that summer was a visit by my brother from Salt Lake, along with our sister's son from Tahoe City. It happened that Ted was away on piloting jobs during most of their visit, but the three of us had a wonderful time. Bill was an experienced outdoorsman familiar with boats and outboard motors. He and Mark fished for salmon, set shrimp and crab pots, and dug clams on our beach, and we hiked into the hills and dug around in the old Indian midden on Indian Island. Their visit was the happiest two weeks I had experienced in years.

Before the summer was over I began to dread the winter and tried to think of some diversions. I had read about the Alaska State Council on the Arts, and the grants they gave to artistic individuals and groups. I applied for a grant to visit high schools in Anchorage and Fairbanks, to talk to would-be writers.

My application was accepted and in November and December I made weeklong lecture trips to both cities. This experience opened an entirely new world to me.

In Fairbanks, Charles Keim, then dean of the School of Journalism at the University of Alaska, took me under his wing. I had read in biographies that writers are a jealous breed, often unfriendly to each other. This certainly was not the case with Chuck Keim. He and his wife Betty took me into their home, and he arranged my appointments and drove me to the schools in Fairbanks.

At the university I met graduate journalism students and instructors and had a chance to talk shop without fear of being accused of pretense or conceit. My isolated existence on the homestead began to seem more barren than ever.

The experience in Anchorage was similar. Some of the students in the audience were genuinely interested, but the teachers asked the most questions. Some of them had come to Alaska for adventure and were already planning to write. I enjoyed the conversations and their attention, which offset the feelings of worthlessness that had been returning in the previous two years.

That winter I worked on a book about our homestead experiences. I made no attempt to gloss over the way we lived, and while I elaborated on some of the highlights, the point of the book was to tell just how our part of Alaska was settled by the homesteaders of the 1940s.

My agent sent me the comments of various editors who read the manuscript and rejected it. One wrote, "This sounds like it wasn't much fun."

Well, dammit, I thought, *it wasn't much fun.* This wasn't a *We Took to the Woods* book, or *The Egg and I.* I had tried to give an honest account of life in the wilderness. It seemed to me that my experiences could shed some light on the lives of pioneer women in the American West, about which very little had been written. But since my book wasn't entertaining, it wasn't accepted.

Crisis and Decision

THE WINTER of 1970-71 was a crisis season for me.
An unusual number of visitors had come up the bay that
summer and fall—to hunt, to look for land, and to work on
homesites around the lake at the head of Bear Cove. Ted usually went with the hunters for moose and waterfowl. He also
worked hard getting in our winter supply of coal, making
seven trips to the Homer side to dig coal out of the veins
that layered the sandstone cliffs.

In earlier days I had gone with him occasionally, until he
pointed out that he could bring home more coal if my
weight wasn't added to the load. Now I was content to stay
home alone, whatever his errands. In fact, I was glad to be
left behind.

With no one living on the Pomeroy place, I lost my reason for walking over the ridge occasionally as I used to do, to visit Roxy. To get out of the house for exercise, and to have a project of my own, I built a trail through the woods to the top of Moose Point, which separated our place from Newmans' old homestead. From that high spot I could look across Kachemak Bay, to the slopes on top of the Homer bluffs.

Where once the view was nothing but grasslands and patchy woods, now the sun glinted on metal roofs and on an occasional windshield as cars drove along the East Road out of Homer. While Bear Cove was more deserted than when we first arrived, the Homer side was filling up with home-sites and suburban residences. A few years later enough people moved to the head of Kachemak Bay on the Homer side to populate three small villages. Old, remote homesteads were divided into small farms that held dwellings, barns, roads and trails, and hundreds of cattle, which grazed on the Fox River flats.

Soon after returning to Bear Cove we had moved the small warehouse back where Ted built it originally, on the north side of the cabin. Instead of attaching it, he had connected the two buildings with an enclosed porch and now began to finish the interior. He wanted a small study for himself on the far end, with storage shelves and bins near the entrance. The carpenter work interested him and he worked at it every day, planning a ship's room with portholes and a built-in bunk.

That winter was a cold one. Our creeks froze almost to the bottom. We chopped holes ever deeper and dipped the water out. Moisture oozed out of the embankment and reached our coal pile, stacked on the beach above the tide-line. Gradually it glazed over until much of it became sealed in ice and inaccessible. The weather grew too cold for carpenter work and Ted went back to working in the woods.

Although I no longer worked outdoors, the cold depressed me as it continued without a break. It was hard to sleep when frost formed on the blanket around my face, and the groceries stored under my bed slowly froze. We could not keep potatoes and onions, and we shifted case goods around so that the dry goods were stored in the colder areas, with more vulnerable canned supplies nearer to the stove.

Our tiny clearing seemed to revert to the wilderness. I found wolverine tracks not far from the cabin, and we watched two wolves cross a cleared area between the creek and the "house hill." One day a wolverine shambled across the frozen cove.

In the first years of homesteading we had enjoyed good radio programs every evening. "I Love a Mystery," "Information Please," "One Man's Family," "Dragnet," even "The Lone Ranger" and "Sergeant Preston of the Yukon" were favorites. We could count on at least two good programs every night. When we returned to Bear Cove all these programs had disappeared, knocked off the air by television. Since we were out of range of the Anchorage television stations and did not have a steady supply of electricity, we lost out on all outside entertainment. Reading and knitting were my only diversions.

Once again, though, the thing I missed most after the years spent in town was daily mail service. Mail even once a week would have been wonderful, but now we got mail only every three or four weeks, when we chartered a plane to bring it from Homer. Ted found it easier to have the plane land on the beach at Aurora Lagoon, a few miles down Kachemak Bay, than to use the deserted Pomeroy strip. We would arrange by radio for the plane to come and Ted would go down with his skiff and outboard motor to meet the plane, carrying our outgoing mail with him.

As we reverted to the habits of our original homestead days, my spirits fell and courage ebbed. I came to see that for many years my expectations of Ted had been unrealistic. I had been trapped by his enthusiasms and the dreams that seemed so real to him.

Love is not always killed by one great wound. Sometimes it dies of a thousand tiny cuts. Indifference to my thoughts and feelings, little jokes that carried a painful sting, thoughtless teasing that he knew offended me, subtle down-putting when I had reasons for satisfaction, all took their toll. At last I understood that although we had spent 30 years in marriage, we had never truly shared our lives.

That long cold winter, when we had snow until the 20th of May, I finally admitted to myself that we had conducted our lives to suit Ted's dreams, while mine were incidental or nonexistent as far as he was concerned. He dreamed castles in Spain, but could never put foundations under them as Thoreau had recommended. Our reasons for living in the wilderness had proved to be pointless.

For most of my life I had put myself down, always hoping for approval, being shaped by the man in my life, first my father, then Ted. Facile praise and humoring were not what I wanted, but I did crave recognition for my honest accomplishments and respect for my endeavors.

I was 56 years old, with the prospect of living at least 20 more years. To go on as we had been now seemed impossible to me. In a last appeal I suggested we get a place in Homer for the winters and come back to the Cove for the summer months. Ted refused to consider it, and I started to make plans for a life of my own.

The first thing I did was to apply for another grant from the Alaska State Council on the Arts. This time I wanted to go to Nome, Barrow, Fairbanks, Anchorage, Kodiak, Homer, Seldovia, Valdez and Cordova, in three separate trips. When the grant was awarded I was assured of autumn and winter activities and income, whatever else fate had in store. Thoughtfully I made my plans.

I was working on a nonfiction book suggested by my editor at Ives Washburn. In addition to the research material I had already assembled, I planned in-the-field information gathering while on the school lecture trips. A small article sale to *Science of Mind* magazine encouraged me. By this time my first five books had gone out of print, but the eight others still produced royalty checks twice a year.

The weather that summer was cool and damp. Ice formed on the moss on the edge of the creek on June 22, and many mornings were foggy. Fewer strangers came into the Cove. All available waterfront land had been filed on, and the wet weather discouraged campers. Several young men were building a cabin at Loon Lake, and they came occasionally to borrow tools and to send radio messages. For a time we had better mail service, thanks to John and Phyllis Cooper, who came to their summer home on Bear Island nearly every weekend, bringing our mail and any groceries we had ordered by radio.

My outdoor work on the flower gardens around the cabin continued. I remembered Lillian Leonardt's flower beds. All her plants had disappeared, but I felt that I carried on her tradition and Jenny's, by transplanting wildflowers that I found in niches and rock slides all around the Cove.

Ted was engrossed in sluicing down the embankment in front of the cabin and planning the stairway he intended to build, but he also spent a lot of time away from home, making beachcombing trips to Glacier Spit, taking pieces of equipment to Halibut Cove to be repaired by the machinist, traveling to Homer Spit for building materials for the porch roof and sides. He got his first piloting job of the season in the middle of July.

The lumber he had salvaged at Tutka Bay, Port Vita and Seldovia was piled up on various beaches around Bear Cove and near Indian Island, where the Pomeroy group had landed. One day Ted discovered that someone had stolen a part of that stack. He suspected the "hippies" who were drifting into the country at the head of the bay on the Homer side. Someone had evidently come by boat, loaded up a pile of 2 x 8 planks and taken off without being seen.

Of course Ted was furious. He decided to restack the re-maining lumber and chain it together so no one could make off with any more of it. He did not ask for my help and I did not offer it. He seemed as glad as I was to be working alone.

People who saw me during this time later told me they sensed I was desperately unhappy. Apparently my depression also showed in my letters to friends, but Ted did not notice. He left in the morning to be gone all day, and I was glad to be home by myself.

I secretly made my plans and was carrying them out. I would go to Seward, one of the few Kenai Peninsula towns where it was possible to live comfortably without a car. By letter I confided in my friend Pat Williams, who arranged with her mother to rent an apartment to me again in the Ray Building. I would stay in Seward at least until the first of the year, when I had finished my Arts Council grant obligations. Then I would decide on a course to follow for the rest of my life. I was well known in the seafood industry and was confi-dent that even at my age I could find work as a packing plant bookkeeper.

My time to leave Bear Cove was not definite. It would have to be before freeze-up, so a float plane could pick me up at our beach. I intended to take only my books and clothes, but even that much would be awkward for me to take over the ridge to the Pomeroy landing strip in winter, and I didn't want any help from Ted. Since new snow had fallen on the peaks behind Bear Cove before the end of July, my time of departure would probably be some time in September.

Knowing Ted's nature, I would have to be ready to leave when I told him. Nothing would be worse than having to stay even overnight once he knew I was leaving. By the first of August I started to pack.

Ted was preoccupied with his lumber piles, his embankment sluicing and trying to get the tractor running. The machinist from Halibut Cove couldn't find the problem, and Ted finally contacted a heavy equipment man in Homer who came up and located the trouble. As had been the case for a number of years, we were living in our own worlds, with little meaningful communication between us.

I had not decided on a way to tell Ted I was leaving him. With most of my clothes packed or discarded in the garbage pile that he passed every day, I started to fill cartons with my books and papers. These I stacked beside my desk in the living room, silently begging him to ask me what I was up to. He did not notice anything different.

One day toward the end of August he came into the cabin filled with enthusiasm. Now that the tractor was repaired, he was working in a new area he had not paid attention to in previous years. He was beaming.

"I've found the place to build our new home."

My first reaction was despair. I had heard these momentous announcements so many times. Then I wanted to scream. In almost 30 years he had located a dozen or more sites for our home, had even done clearing and excavating. Then he found drawbacks and started searching anew for the perfect site. This latest discovery would be no different.

The next day some insignificant difference came up between us. I can't remember what it was, but he was startled

191

when I disagreed with him. "What's wrong with you?" he demanded. "You're acting so different."

For a moment I hesitated, wondering whether this was the time. Then I told him I was unhappy.

"I suppose you hate me," he said accusingly.

"I don't hate you, Ted," I replied without rancor. "I hate Bear Cove."

"Then go," he snapped. "I'll call a plane for you."

He strode across the room to the short-wave radio.

"Wait! I'll do it myself when I'm ready."

He left the cabin and I finished packing. He heard me call the air taxi operator and spoke to me from the porch steps. The mountains beyond the distant side of Bear Cove were silhouetted against a towering bank of sunlit, glowing cloud. He pointed.

"I hope the life you make for yourself will be as beautiful as that sky."

His voice was thick with unshed tears. My own throat tightened as I watched him stride across the clearing and disappear into the surrounding forest.

My final packing did not take long. I carried 14 suitcases and cardboard boxes down the perilous trail to the water's edge. Within an hour I was on the plane, my life at Bear Cove ended. I moved on to an uncertain, different, but ultimately happier life.

Epilog

FROM THE *Anchorage Daily News*, Sept. 19, 1993, under Elsa Pedersen's byline and the heading "50 Years on the Kenai / A half-century of Alaska wears the body—but not the spirit":

> *NOTE TO THE EDITOR: To date I have written 105 "General Delivery" columns published in We Alaskans, beginning March 1, 1980 (your second issue). My second column, a month later, was headlined "Growing Older In Alaska" and described my feelings at applying for the Longevity Bonus. This month (on Sept. 26) I will celebrate my arrival in Alaska a half-century ago. Fifty years! Where have they gone? And who is that old white-haired woman I see in the mirror every morning?*

STERLING—Who coined the phrase "the golden years"? I doubt if it was an older person, or that it applied to anyone more than a few years older than 60.

Walt and I were married in our mid-50s and had no illusions about growing old. In fact, we planned for it. Walt built us a small, super-insulated house on the edge of a lake at the end of his land most distant from the highway. We heat with wood that we buy cut to length, plus green wood brought to us by good neighbors as they enlarge and landscape their property. We've never had a frozen pipe, and only routine maintenance has been required so far.

What we didn't count on was that our bodies would give out. When we were young no one thought about industrial physical protection. Walt operated a rock crusher when the Sterling Highway was built, without a dust mask, ear plugs or any other safety devices. He ran a tractor and loader on his own land and for others, over rough ground that jarred his bones. He cleared acres of land with chain saws, again without protection from sawdust or noise. No wonder his hearing is failing now.

My own history was equally rigorous for a woman. On a

remote homestead at the head of Kachemak Bay, I worked at one end of a crosscut saw as my first husband and I cleared seven acres of old-growth forest. I chopped wood, dug a garden, and one summer dug out an embankment behind the cabin, 50 feet long, 6 feet wide and 12 feet high at the highest point.

For years we did not know how we were punishing our bodies, just as other Alaska homesteaders have done over the years. Now, as we approach 80 years old, we are paying the price.

We are often surprised when it takes us so long to do a piece of work we used to do in a jiffy. It's hard to understand why our backs ache, why it's hard to get down on our knees, why we have to stop and rest or put off to another day finishing a task we used to do in a few hours. We get impatient with ourselves that it takes us so long to get organized to accomplish a simple project.

I have given up flower gardens, only maintaining the beds that are planted with perennials that grow and bloom with a minimum of care. This is the last year I'll grow greenhouse tomatoes, since we can now buy them Alaska-grown. I don't bake bread very often and our meals are increasingly simple.

We do enjoy driving and are pleased that the new highway to Soldotna has 8-foot-wide paved shoulders, so we can pull off anywhere to let impatient drivers go by.

So far we're still flying. We've had some good trips this summer, over the Harding Icefield to the Pacific, across Cook Inlet to the beautiful Redoubt Flats and the foothills of the Chigmit Mountains. It's getting harder, though, to fold our old bones into the two-seat plane.

Getting old means giving up one thing after another. My prayer is that we're never reduced to just sitting and rocking.

Elsa Pedersen is a free-lance writer who lives in Sterling.

ELSA AND WALT Pedersen at their home in Sterling, Alaska, about 1981.
Photo courtesy of Kathleen Pedersen Haley.

WALT PEDERSEN died at Sterling on March 14, 1998, after writing his own forthright obituary for the *Peninsula Clarion*. The October 1998 issue of *Trumpetings Online*, a publication of the Trumpeter Swan Society (Vol. VIII, No. 3), noted: "The Society has lost a long-time member and true friend. I recently received a note from Elsa Pedersen, telling me that her husband Walt had passed away earlier in the year. Walt and Elsa hosted a number of us on their Sterling, Alaska, homestead during the 6th Trumpeter Swan Society Conference held in Anchorage in September 1978. Walt graciously toured us in his float plane over the Kenai National Moose Range to see nesting Trumpeters on many of the refuge lakes.

"As a fitting eulogy, for the first time, a pair of Trumpeters nested on Walt and Elsa's lake this past spring and hatched five cygnets. Our heartfelt sympathies go out to

Elsa. We valued Walt's friendship, his support of the Society, and, of course, his keen interest in Trumpeter Swans. – Dave Weaver."

Ted Pedersen died in Homer in 1990. His photographs and other records, including several biographical accounts on film and videotape, are in the state archives in Juneau. The book about his and Walt's sea-captain father was never written. Laura Tyson, Walt Pedersen's first wife, died on Christmas Day 1992 in Sterling. She had continued to operate the Moose River resort she and Walt built in the early years, and as Laura Pedersen she wrote a column on home-steading for *The Alaskan Quarterly*. She also had served as postmaster for the community of Naptowne, now Sterling.

AS THIS BOOK is readied for publication, Elsa Pedersen's life is ebbing. She has had scant time or patience in her 86 years for "sitting and rocking," and after the recent sudden onset of a debilitating illness she refused life-prolonging hospital measures and asked to be taken back to the Sterling homestead, where she had lived alone since Walt's death. "It's time," she said. "I'm tired." Her stepdaughter, Kathleen Pedersen Haley, and longtime friend Susan Gilbertson are with her, and other friends come and go or send greetings and reminiscences to be read and relished. Susan's youngest son and Elsa have always been close, and his presence is a particular joy. She is pleased with the progress of her last book.

Neighbors like to tell the story of Walt's christening the lake he built on the homestead after he and Elsa were married. "Safin Lake" is the name, for "Sex After Fifty Is Nifty." A few days ago Elsa chuckled with a visitor over that recollection. Later she mused, "The lake is frozen, isn't it? You'll have to wait till spring to scatter our ashes."

This index is drawn from Elsa Pedersen's memoir. The Publisher's Note and Epilog are not included.

Kachemak Bay Years

Project coordinator and editor: Jackie Pels

Design and production: David R. Johnson

Illustrations: Rebecca Poulson, Sitka, Alaska, www.theoutercoast.com

Thanks to Lee Poleske and Patricia Williams of the Resurrection Bay
Historical Society for their commitment to Elsa Pedersen's story;
to Leslie Pels-Beck and Barbara White, who read and commented on the
original typescript, and to Werner Pels, who scanned it into publishable
format; to librarian Rose Welton for Cataloging-in-Publication data;
and to Dori Lynn Anderson of the *Peninsula Clarion,* Peggy Petersen
Arness, Gary Bogue, Janet Klein, Marge Mullen, Alice Nilson,
Jan O'Meara, Susan Springer, and librarians Lynn Hallquist of the
Anchorage Daily News and Deborah Mole of the University of Alaska
Anchorage, for aid in research. (Portions of Elsa Pedersen's unpublished
memoir appeared in Susan Woodward Springer's *Seldovia, Alaska / An
Historical Portrait of Life in Herring Bay*, Blue Willow, Inc., 1997.)
Special thanks to Susan Gilbertson, Kathleen Pedersen Haley and
Pat Williams for gathering photos and memories at a difficult time.

Composition by Archetype Typography, Berkeley, Calif.

Printed at Inkworks Press, Berkeley, Calif.

Alkaline pH recycled paper (Solutions by Nekoosa)

Hardscratch Press
2358 Banbury Place, Walnut Creek, CA 94598-2347
phone/fax 925/935-3422